KV-625-807

...returned on or
...ate stamped below.

PEROWNE, STEWART
HOLY PLACES OF CHRISTENDOM.
STEWART, PEROWNE.
246.909

30130503923289

OR 14.9.93

HOLY PLACES OF CHRISTENDOM

Stewart Perowne

COLLEGE LIBRARY
COLLEGE OF TECHNOLOGY
CARNARVON ROAD
SOUTHEND-ON-SEA, ESSEX

Mowbrays LONDON AND OXFORD

270

BT 76490

To John
Bishop of Fulham and Gibraltar

Frontispiece. A panoramic view of Jerusalem.

Endpapers. A thirteenth century pilgrims' itinerary from England to the Holy Land. (Old Royal Library MS 14 CVII f2, by permission of the British Library Board.)

© 1976 A. R. Mowbray & Co. Limited
First published in 1976 by A. R. Mowbray & Co. Limited.
The Alden Press. Osney Mead, Oxford OX2 OEG ISBN: 0 264 66057 9
Printed in Great Britain, by Redwood Burn International, Trowbridge, Wiltshire

Contents

Introduction 7

1 'Unto us a Son is born' 11

2 The Holy City 25

3 Galilee 33

4 The Way of the Cross 45

5 The Holy Sepulchre 59

6 'First Fruits of the Spirit' 73

7 Paul: the Apostle to the Gentiles 81

8 Caesars and Saints 93

9 Monks and Missionaries 103

10 'Then longen folk to goon on pilgrimages' 123

11 'The One Remains' 143

List of illustrations 157

Acknowledgements 159

Index 159

eo inuenies uidere abaham et ilce ma ... nibjeim no ... supheste

EGO SVM DEVS. BETHEL. VBI. VHYISTI. LAPIDE.

Introduction

'THE DESIRE to be a pilgrim is deeply rooted in human nature. To stand where those that we reverence once stood, to see the very sites where they were born and toiled and died, gives us a feeling of mystical contact with them and is a practical expression of our homage. And if great men of the world have their shrines to which their admirers come from afar, still more do men flock eagerly to those places where, they believe, the Divine has sanctified the earth.' (Runciman, *A History of the Crusades*, Vol. I, ch. 3.)

It is those very places, sanctified by the Divine, that merit the name of 'Holy Places'; but whence came the transcendental concept of God, one and only, which was to be the foundation of the Christian idea of 'the holy' and to be the *raison d'être* of the Holy Places of Christendom?

Ten miles north of Jerusalem there is a little village called Beitin, of old Bethel, but originally Luz. To this obscure hamlet there came, as related in the book of Genesis (28.11) the Patriarch Jacob. Laying his head on a heap of the silver-grey stones which abound there, he fell asleep, and as he slept he dreamed. In his dream he saw angels going up and down a ladder, stretched between heaven and earth. Above it stood the Lord, who spoke words of comfort and promise to the sleeper. When Jacob woke up, he exclaimed: 'Surely the Lord is in this place, and I knew it not. How dreadful is this place.' Which is just what anyone might have said who had had such a dream in such a setting: clearly Bethel was, by the canons of universal primitive religion, a 'holy place'.

The idea of holiness both of spirit and place is as old as man himself. From his first consciousness he was aware that his actions were always conditioned and frequently frustrated by a power, or rather powers, beyond himself. The manifestations of this extra-human potency were of two opposed kinds, the one friendly, the other hostile. A friendly power sent the sunshine and the rain to nourish the children of men, a hostile power sent hail and earthquake to destroy them. When man took to the sea, he might be sped on his way by a favouring breeze or wrecked by a hurricane.

1. 'Jacob's Ladder', a twelfth-century Byzantine manuscript illumination showing angels ascending and descending over the sleeping Jacob at Bethel.

How bewildering, how unaccountable these powers were, now benign, now spiteful, according to no apparent rule.

It was clear from the beginning that if man was to survive, two things must be done. First every effort must be made to find out what the powers intended; secondly every possible step must be taken to ensure their continual favour or to avert their wrath. It was from these twin necessities that primitive religion grew, and by twin means it was practised, namely by oracles and offerings. But where was it most propitious to celebrate these essential rites? Some of the powers already possessed natural and obvious habitations. Springs, for instance, so alive and bountiful, must clearly be the abode of kindly spirits, and to them thank-offerings must be duly made; whereas localities blasted by the lightning were clearly the victims of spiteful powers, who must at all costs be propitiated. Gradually it was realized that for the dual purpose of oracle and offering some ampler and more permanent premises were required. Thus was born the idea of the material shrine. If men now dwelt in a house, surely these powers – it is time to call them gods – must be furnished with a dwelling-place, with a temple in fact.

Let us now go back to Bethel. It is the second half of the verse already cited that has made Bethel for ever unique, for Jacob goes on to say: 'This is none other than the house of God (Beth-el, in Hebrew), and this is the gate of heaven.' The stones of Bethel were to form the foundation of every Christian 'Holy Place', the visible and actual link between man and God. With the concentration of Jewish worship in the one and only Temple of the one and only God in Jerusalem, Bethel like its neighbour Shiloh lost its status of shrine, but it still retains something of its meaning amid the Judaean hills.

It was into this climate of belief that Jesus was born, into a system of worship centred in Jerusalem, a system which combined the ancient cult of offering with the ancient cult of seeking to ascertain the divine will, but all now elevated and transmuted into service of the One, supreme, invisible and almighty. What did the ministry of Jesus make of this system? The story of his ministry is given in the Gospels, and it is wisest to take the story from them, as it was told. There is Jesus, always on the move, always, it seems, doing two things. First, he is working all the good he can for his fellow men and women. He heals, he comforts, he exhorts. Secondly he denounces the apathetic materialism of his age, the age of a land restless under the rule of an alien and pagan Rome, then at the zenith of its political dominion.

The story, read and understood in unbroken continuity, conveys a remarkable sense of balance. We begin with events before the birth of Jesus, then we learn of his birth, of his youth, of his brief ministry, of his death, of his resurrection, and ascension. It was this life, lived against the 'eternal landscape of the past' that enables us to contemplate, to venerate, and to draw strength from the Holy Places of Christendom, first of all those places hallowed by physical contact with Jesus, and then with so many others in lands of the east and of the west which, in perpetual commemoration of his life, have been sanctified by the Divine.

2. Bethel looking towards Ai the scene of Joshua's great victory after the capture of Jericho. On the left the ruins of the primitive sanctuary.

1 'Unto us a Son is born'

4 *top*. The Greek Orthodox Church of the Annunciation in Nazareth showing the crypt and Mary's Well.

5 *above*. Greek Catholic Synagogue-Church.

3 *opposite*. Nazareth, a general view showing in the background the Mount of Precipitation.

CHILDHOOD STORIES are rare in antiquity. This makes the tale of the infancy of Jesus all the more interesting. But besides the narrative of his birth and boyhood, we even have the story of events which preceded and as it were led up to his birth, because Luke gives us the narrative of the Annunciation, and the Visitation, and the fullest story of the Nativity.

In virtue of Luke's testimony Nazareth, which Mark mentions not at all, Matthew only after the Return from Egypt, and John at the outset of Jesus' ministry, became of cardinal importance to those who wished to follow the life of the Master. It was here that the life was foretold. Nazareth ought therefore (we might reason) to possess the most ancient church in all the Holy Land. In fact the one whose soaring cupola now dominates the town was only completed in 1966. There are two other churches in Nazareth, both of great antiquity, but neither is outwardly impressive. The reason for this comparative and admittedly disappointing obscurity is historical. Eastern tradition places the Annunciation not, as in western lore, following Luke 1.23, in the house of Mary, but by the town well. The actual source of the fountain lies 162 yards to the north-west of the outlet. This was the original sacred site of Nazareth, and a church was built hard by as soon as the Christians were able to acquire it. That was in the seventh century. This sanctuary, known as St Gabriel's, now forms the crypt of the Orthodox church. The upper church, as with so many such Orthodox churches, is in the form of a simple rectangle, forty-eight feet square. This building is only two centuries old. It is now known to the Orthodox as the Church of the Annunciation, or simply as Mary's House. Consecrated water may still be drawn from the well in the crypt.

The other holy site apart from the great basilica is the traditional one of the Synagogue in which Jesus learned his letters, and himself taught, and from which he was ejected, as told in Luke 4. 16–30. It was acquired by the Franciscans in 1741 and by them handed over to the Greek Catholics thirty years later.

6. 'Ain Karim, a general view of the town where Mary visited her cousin Elizabeth. The Church of Saint John is in the middle of the picture.

The great, grand Roman Catholic church, modern though it be, stands on a site of venerable antiquity. Excavations carried out since 1955 have shown that there was a church here in the fifth century, and that below the mosaic floor of that church there are remains of a still earlier building. This building appears to have been a church-synagogue, used by a community of Judaeo-Christians such as we should expect to find in this predominantly Jewish town, from which the Jews were only excluded in the year 630.

There was a Byzantine church here, designed to hallow the house of Mary. This was succeeded by a Crusader church. After the expulsion of the Latins the site lay desolate, until in 1730 the Franciscans obtained leave from the Turks to erect a church of sorts on it. Hastily, that is before some opponent or rival could bribe the Porte to cancel its permission, the Franciscans did build a makeshift church, not even correctly orientated. This was enlarged in 1870 (fourteen years after the issue of the Edict of Toleration) and demolished in 1955. The new, imposing church was begun in 1960.

We must now go with Mary to visit her cousin Elizabeth in the village called 'Ain Karim, that is 'Vineyard Spring', four miles west of Jerusalem. In the first chapter of Luke's Gospel old Zachary, on duty in the Temple, is vouchsafed

7. Church of the Visitation, 'Ain
Karim. The Grotto and Cistern.

a vision of Gabriel, who tells him that he and his wife
Elizabeth, old as they both are, shall be the parents of John
the Baptist. Zachary is struck dumb. Gabriel's promise was
fulfilled. Elizabeth was in her sixth month when her cousin
Mary from Nazareth came to see her and to tell her her own
good news. Alone of Judaean villages 'Ain Karim is of an
almost Italian gentleness. The brilliant green patchwork of
its gardens, nourished by the glistening and perennial rills,
is framed by the surrounding crags, their severity now
tempered by terrace above terrace of pine, cypress, olive,
apricot and fig. You could not devise a more welcoming
milieu for the reunion of Elizabeth, soon to become the
mother of John the Baptist, and Mary.

In 'Ain Karim up on the hill there is one church which
commemorates John in the Wilderness (Loneliness is a
more accurate rendering of the Greek). In the village below
there are two more. The first is also dedicated to the Baptist,
and to his father Zachary. There was a Byzantine chapel
here, and then a Crusader church. As so often, there are
grotto-chapels below.

The Franciscans acquired the site in 1621, but only in
1674 were they able to reside here permanently. The present
church dates from the last six years of the nineteenth
century. Here is commemorated Zachary's immortal hymn:
Benedictus, 'Blessed be the Lord God of Israel, for he hath
visited and redeemed his people.'

13

The second and more important church is also Franciscan property; and it was from this dwelling there sounded forth to mankind one of the most heartlifting hymns ever uttered. *Magnificat anima mea Dominum*, 'my soul doth magnify the Lord' sang Mary. Here it may be appropriate to say a word about the Franciscans in the Holy Land. They first arrived in the thirteenth century, Saint Francis having himself visited Cairo and called upon the Sultan al-Kamil in 1219. In 1247 the Egyptians regained control of Jerusalem, which they had held in pre-Crusader days. During the five centuries following the fall of Acre, the last Crusading foothold in the Holy Land, in 1291, it was the Franciscans who did all in their power to safeguard the Holy Places of their Faith. Their Superior was called, as he still is, Most Reverend Father Custodian of the Holy Land.

It was only with the advent of the British in 1917, and during the thirty years of their even-handed administration, that the Franciscans were at last free to build and rebuild on their sacred sites. By a providential conjunction they then had at their behest a dedicated architect of genius, Antonio Barluzzi. Wherever Barluzzi built or restored he made his plan conform to and proclaim the event which the particular church commemorated.

And so to Bethlehem.

Of all the shrines of the Holy Land, Bethlehem is the most magnetic. First, there is its position, on that gaunt ridge, five miles south of Jerusalem, three thousand feet above the Mediterranean Sea to the west, more than four thousand above the pewter-hued waters of the Dead Sea to the east. In the foreground looms the sinister cone of the palace-tomb of Herod the Great, who had brought such anguish upon Bethlehem; and in the far distant region of the dawn the long level line of the Mountains of Moab is stretched from Nebo to Arnon like a backcloth.

Until the mid-nineteenth century, the little town was much as it had always been, the ancient city of David huddled round the great basilica.

The basilica is still the heart and focus of the whole composition. To start with it is by far the most majestic of the primitive churches, of which it is also the most complete. Secondly it is unique in harbouring convents not only of the Orthodox and Latins (as the Roman Catholic Church is known in the Levant) but of the Armenians as well, whose national Church is older by a generation than that of imperial and Christian Rome. This ecumenical synthesis is delightfully realized by the annual celebration here in the

8. Church of the Visitation, 'Ain Karim.

birthplace of Jesus, not of one Christmas, but of three. First comes the Western Feast, on the 24/25 December; then, twelve days later, that of the Orthodox Church which here in Bethlehem still observes the Old Style calendar; and then on 17/18 January the Armenians keep the Feast of the Nativity combined with the Epiphany. The Epiphany is the older solemnity. Christmas was adapted from the Roman Saturnalia, and at first combined with the Epiphany. It was apparently only separated from it in the fourth century, when Saint Jerome brought the date, 25 December, with him from Rome.

There were churches in Palestine before the one at Bethlehem; but they all perished during the appalling devastation wrought by the invading Persians in the year 614, a catastrophe from which Palestine never really recovered. The Bethlehem church alone escaped because on the tympanum above the western portal there was a mosaic (like that which still adorns Rome's oldest standing church, Santa Maria in Trastevere, which shows both Jerusalem and Bethlehem) depicting the Three Kings in Persian dress. This tribute to national pride saved this church, and this church alone, from destruction. The church we now behold is not the original building, but it is substantially a sixth-century restoration of the original.

When in the year 326 Constantine's saintly mother, the empress Helena, was in Palestine, she commanded that a church be built on the site of the birthplace. This was easily identified because, in the first quarter of the second century, the emperor Hadrian in an endeavour to obliterate any memory or vestige of Jewish and Christian cults had planted over the cave-stable a shrine of Adonis, Adonis being the lover of Venus, patroness of Rome, and himself worshipped in a cave up in Syria. But Christians still venerated the birthplace of their Saviour, as in the middle of the second century Justin Martyr, a Palestinian, bears witness.

Constantine at his mother's bidding raised a magnificent shrine over the Grotto. All that remains to us of this building as it originally stood are some fine mosaics two feet below the present floor. In or about the year 540, Justinian had the whole church rebuilt, using the old materials.

Besides being hallowed by the Nativity of Christ, Bethlehem acquired a secondary but highly important fame in the fifth century, for it was here that the already renowned Jerome settled with his pious Roman ladies to pursue his biblical studies which resulted in the Vulgate, still the official Latin Bible of the Roman Catholic Church.

After the Muslim conquest Christian worship was still tolerated; but by 808 when Charlemagne called for a report

9. Christmas procession leaving the Basilica of the Nativity at Bethlehem. On the right is the Armenian convent and on the extreme left the Roman Catholic Church of Saint Catherine.

10 *opposite*. The interior of the Basilica of the Nativity.

on monasteries in the Holy Land, in place of the five which had flourished in Bethlehem in the seventh century there was now but one community of fifteen religious, plus two anchorites who sat on the tops of pillars like Saint Simeon Stylites.

With the coming of the Crusaders in 1099 security returned, closely followed by prosperity. A community of Augustinian canons was installed here, as in the Holy Sepulchre, and Greek and Latin clergy lived and worshipped together in amity. In the year 1101, Baldwin, first Crusader king of Jerusalem, was crowned here, because he would not receive a temporal crown in the city where his Master had been crowned with thorns. In 1109 the basilica was raised to the status of cathedral. Endowments poured in from as far away even as Scotland. In the middle of the century a general redecoration was put in hand. In 1158 Baldwin III married the daughter of the Byzantine emperor, Manuel Commenos, so that both Byzantine and western artists were employed when Baldwin's successor Amaury undertook the restoration between 1161 and 1169. Parts of the exquisite mosaics which were then dedicated still glimmer from the upper walls. On the pillars may be descried armorial bearings, mostly German, and paintings of saints, done about 1130, an amicable company drawn from the west and north no less than from the east. One of these pictures shows Saint James, now patron of Compostela in Spain, with a pilgrim kneeling at his feet, with his pointed shoes and the scrip with a shell on it (the shell is also sometimes shown worn on the hat). He recalls here in Bethlehem the pilgrim of whom the mad Ophelia sings in Hamlet: 'You can tell him by his cockle hat and staff, and his sandalled shoon.'

The great western facade of the basilica has been progressively attenuated, in the quest for security, and to prevent the passage of horses and mules sent to carry off marbles stripped from the walls for use elsewhere. We enter, therefore, by a tiny door six feet high. Passing through the *narthex* we stand at last, astounded, in the basilica itself. It is best to move at once to the south wall, and thence to contemplate the forest of rose-coloured marble monoliths. There are forty of them, ten in each row, not counting the terminal pilasters. A great monolithic font of the same stone is the only object that breaks the symmetry of the colonnades.

11 *lower left*. A painted column in the interior of the Church of the Nativity.

12 *lower right*. Entrance to the Church of the Nativity at Bethlehem which was deliberately reduced as a 'security measure' against marauders.

And so at last we come to the Grotto, down below what is now the crossing, past the Armenian, Coptic and Assyrian altars in the north transept, and down the little Crusader stairway, the columns marked with the souvenir crosses of

13 *above*. The Crusader Steps down to the Grotto.

14 *opposite*. The Grotto of the Nativity. In the centre of the picture is the altar of the Nativity above the place where Jesus was born. On the right is the Chapel of the Manger.

so many nameless and humble men and women who have reached this goal of their pilgrimage. The Grotto is embellished with costly hangings and many a silver lamp. But it has been like that for centuries. Jerome wished the silver coverings away: perhaps we may do the same. But the very fact that he did so is a guarantee that the little shrine is much as it was sixteen hundred years ago. At the eastern end of it

is a niche, in the floor of which is a silver star proclaiming that it was here that Jesus was born. (The story that it was a squabble over this star which brought on the Crimean war is a figment. The dispute had been settled months before the war broke out.) On the right, just as described by the very earliest pilgrims, there is the manger, also richly adorned.

At the Christmas celebrations the little chapel is crammed to suffocation. The best time to visit it is in the dusk of an ordinary day. Then come the Franciscan fathers, with their young attendants. They sing their simple devotions, and go again about their daily tasks. The visitor feels comforted and perhaps a bit stronger from the experience; for whatever we may believe or disbelieve, it is impossible not to be moved by this little cave, loved and venerated by so many for so long; because here we are standing in the very first Christian nursery.

We may leave the shrine by way of the Franciscan church of Saint Catherine. The cloisters, sensitively restored by Barluzzi, now display clustered columns with capitals decorated with foliage or grotesques typical of French work of the twelfth century. Down below is a series of caves, one of which is venerated as 'the study of Saint Jerome'. In the western wall of this cloister-garth is a door which gives access to what was once part of Justinian's *narthex*. It later became the base of the Crusader bell-tower. The walls of the little chamber are decorated with twelfth-century frescoes in the Byzantine style, depicting the Holy Family and saints with their traditional attributes. These paintings, which only came to light some thirty years ago, are unique.

15. Star which denotes the site of the sacred birth

2 The Holy City

FROM THE penumbra of the Bethlehem basilica we come out into the crystalline light of the Palestine day. On our left is the great cliff of the Armenian convent, with that of the Orthodox beyond it. On our right, that is to the north, there is a precipice, above which once stood the Augustinian church alongside the basilica itself. The site is now occupied by the Franciscan church. To the west of the main square is the Syrian church of Saint Mary, the Lutheran church with its conical spire, and the gay Assyrian shrine.

Down below in the plain which lies between us and Jerusalem are to be seen the vestiges of a Byzantine church which commemorated the Shepherds – there is a modern one near by – to whom the angels proclaimed glory to God in the highest and peace to men of goodwill. No scene in all the Life is more familiar than this, from the triumphant chorus of Handel's *Messiah*, and from countless representations in painting and sculpture.

17 *right*. 'Adoration of the Magi' by Hieronymus Bosch in the Prado, Madrid.

16 *opposite*. The 'Shepherds' Fields' below Bethlehem looking east towards the Wilderness of Judaea and the Mountains of Moab.

The Jerusalem Temple is the scene of the next episode in the Infancy, namely the Purification of Mary. While the ceremony was being performed the aged Simeon took the child in his arms and uttered our third great canticle, *Nunc Dimittis*, 'Lord now lettest thou thy servant depart in peace according to thy word.'

This happened in the Temple, which was thus for the first time hallowed, as it would more than once be hallowed afterwards, as a Christian Holy Place. The concept of the Temple as a Christian Holy Place may not leap to the mind. Its associations with Judaism as the unique and sole early centre of the Jewish faith, and the unparalleled splendour of

18. Jerusalem, with the Dome of the Rock Mosque in the middle of the Temple platform, and, to the right, the Kedron Valley.

19. Inside the Dome of the Rock showing the place on which, by tradition, Abraham prepared to sacrifice Isaac. It was also the site of Araunah the Jebusite's threshing floor over which Solomon built his first temple. According to some scholars, this sacred rock once bore the sacrificial altar of the Temple. Muslims hold that from this rock Muhammad ascended to heaven, hence the importance to them also of the Holy City.

the Dome of the Rock and the Aqsa mosque which ranks after Mecca and Medina as the third (originally first) Holy Place of Islam – these associations can easily overlay the idea of the Temple as a Christian site. In fact no other single locality has such repeated and manifold physical connections with Jesus – in infancy, in boyhood and up to the very last week of his ministry.

The Temple as Jesus, his parents, relatives and disciples knew it, was the magnificent creation of Herod the Great. The original Temple was built by Solomon in about 960 BC on the threshing-floor of Araunah the Jebusite, itself traditionally the Mount Moriah of Abraham's sacrifice.

28

БЄГ҃ТО ІН҃ССОВО ВО ЄГѴПЕ.

21 *top.* 'Flight into Egypt', a fresco from Bellieu Church in Bulgaria.

22 *above.* The well in a cave, now part of the Church of St Sergius, in Old Cairo, traditionally a resting-place for the Holy Family on the 'Flight into Egypt'.

20 *opposite.* The Western or Wailing Wall, the only visible relic of Herod's Temple as it was in the days of Jesus.

In 597 BC Nebuchadnezzar of Babylon despoiled Jerusalem, and in 588 the city and Temple were destroyed, and the Captivity began. This was ended by Cyrus the Persian in 537. A second Temple was dedicated in 516, but it was in no wise as magnificent as its predecessor. Herod undertook a complete reconstruction not only of the shrine itself (of which the dimensions were sacrosanct) but of the entire precinct. The whole area is no less than thirty-five acres in extent.

This was the splendid work which gave a unique lustre to Jerusalem, so that the Roman encyclopaedist Pliny could describe Jerusalem as 'the finest city not only of Judaea, but of the whole Levant'.

The notion that Jesus was brought up in a small and obscure village and in comparative poverty is false. To start with Nazareth was not obscure. It stood on a pleasant scarp just above one of the world's busiest highways, the Way of the Sea, which joined Egypt and Syria, Alexandria and Antioch, themselves the twin beacons of the Hellenistic Age. Commerce and news were constantly passing up and down beneath the borders of Nazareth. Secondly, Joseph's furniture business must have been lucrative. We have already seen how Mary could go off and visit her cousin without any hesitation. After the birth of Jesus the family lived for a time in a house (Matt. 2.11) in Bethlehem. Later, they migrated to Egypt and later still returned to Nazareth.

29

The next Holy Place to figure in the Life is yet again 'not made with hands'. It is the River Jordan which rises on the southern slopes of Mount Hermon, and then, passing through the Sea of Galilee itself nearly 700 feet below sea level, winds down its serpentine course to the Dead Sea, 1300 feet below. It was over Jordan River that Moses had looked upon the promised land he was never to enter. And it was in this very stream that John, son of Zachary and Elizabeth and cousin of Jesus, started his mission of baptism to repentance, which was to see the commissioning of Jesus at the outset of his ministry. Jesus was then, so Luke tells us (3.23), about thirty.

The mission of John the Baptist created a great stir: it attracted people from all over the country, high and low alike. Bethabara was the place where John was baptizing. Bethabara means the 'house of the ford'. The ford he had chosen in that locality was ideal for his purpose. It lies right on the main highway between Jerusalem and Philadelphia,

23 *above*. Pope Paul VI at Bethabara, the house of the ford, where Saint John the Baptist baptized Jesus.

24 *opposite above*. The Mount of Temptation above Jericho, one of the fortresses of Herod the Great commanding the Jordan Valley.

25 *opposite below*. The view from the Mount of Temptation over the Jordan and the Wilderness of Judaea.

now Amman. The river is broad there, and quite shallow: men and beasts can and do wade through it with ease.

The baptism of Jesus became the starting point of his ministry. Just as in the west the Epiphany, or 'Manifestation' of Jesus to those outside his family, that is to mankind in general, is associated with the visit of the Three Kings, so in the eastern Churches it is always linked with the Baptism.

Immediately after his baptism, Jesus retired to the wilderness near by, and there spent forty days, during which he was tempted by the Devil. There is a mountain above Jericho called 'the Mount of Temptation'.

In our quest for Holy Places we find some that are beyond question 'genuine' in the sense that they were the scenes of actual events. Such are Bethlehem, Nazareth, the Temple, the River Jordan. Others commemorate acts and words only: they provide us with a focus for our recollection and veneration. We may meet many, and find them very helpful. Of such, for many of us, is the Mount of Temptation.

31

3 Galilee

TO GALILEE Jesus returned. He did not linger at Nazareth. After one appearance in the synagogue, during which Jesus made it quite clear whose side he was on, that of the poor and downtrodden, with a marked Gentile bias, he was forcibly bidden to leave. Leave he did and went down to the Lake of Galilee.

The lakeside, besides being beautiful, was far more cosmopolitan, more tolerant, than Nazareth. The international Way of the Sea passed along the western shore of the Lake.

The chief and most cosmopolitan town of all was Capernaum, the centre of Roman government and taxation in Galilee. It harboured a garrison together with a large staff of revenue-officers. We know from Luke 7.5, that one of the Roman centurions was the friend of the Jewish population and had built them a synagogue. The remains of the synagogue have survived. It was in this town that Jesus now established his headquarters with his mother and the rest of the family except Joseph, whose profession kept him at Nazareth.

27 *right*. Capernaum, where Jesus taught, birthplace of Peter and Andrew. These ruins of a synagogue date from the second century.

26 *opposite*. The Sea of Galilee.

28 *above*. Cana of Galilee, scene
of the miracle of the turning
of water into wine.

29 *above right*. 'The Woman of
Samaria', a twelfth-century fresco in
Saint Martin's Church, Zillis,
Switzerland. The representation of the
well is so accurate that it seems
probable that it was made by or at
the dictation of a returned pilgrim.

30 *below right*. Jacob's Well near
Sychar, Samaria, where Jesus met the
woman at the well.

Before the move was made Jesus had visited a village
called Cana, five miles on the road to the Lake, and not far
from the former capital Sepphoris, now Seffuriyeh. It was
from Cana that Nathaniel, one of his earliest and most
faithful disciples, came. Nathaniel scouted the idea that
'any good thing could come out of Nazareth', but Jesus took
to him, and so it was in Nathaniel's town that the 'beginning
of miracles', the transformation of water into nuptial wine,
took place. Some time later (John 4.46) Jesus was at Cana
again; and a leading government officer came up from
Capernaum to beg him to come and heal his son, who was
at the point of death. Jesus assured him that his son would
live. At the very hour that Jesus gave this assurance the lad
started to get better.

Thus Cana, the site of Jesus' first two miracles, very early
became a centre of veneration. There are now two churches
there. The Latin church is a modern shrine consecrated in
1905, above a crypt which may well go back to the fourth
century. The Orthodox church is a simple but dignified
building framed by noble cypresses.

The discourse of Jesus with the woman of Samaria, is said to have taken place as Jesus was returning to Cana from Jerusalem with his disciples. This interchange between Jesus and the unknown woman sustained an exchange of ideas, an exchange on two planes, literal on the part of the woman, spiritual on that of Jesus. The well itself is situated 300 yards south-east of the ruins of Balata, hard by Sychar, now 'Askar.

It is easy to understand why this site early became a holy place for Christians. In the year 333 a visitor known as 'The Bordeaux Pilgrim' mentions a sanctuary, which from his description was clearly a baptistry, a 'sacred pool' as he calls it, but by the end of the tenth century this baptistry-church had been destroyed. The Crusaders raised a new church on the spot in 1130 though with the end of the Latin occupation, this church too fell into ruin. All we see today is the truncated stump of a church never completed. But the well, 162 feet in depth, is still there, and so is the water which refreshed Jesus as he talked with the woman of Samaria.

The whole ministry of Jesus was marked by mobility. He was ever on the move, because, as he himself said (Matthew 8.20), he had no abiding resting-place. He even went as far north as the opulent region about Tyre and its equally proud sister-city, Sidon (Matthew 15.21; Mark 7.31).

Although Capernaum is mentioned so often in the Gospels, more often than any other town save only Jerusalem, apart from the synagogue of which the actual vestiges may be rather later than the days of Jesus, only one small shrine has left us any trace, and that is the so-called house-church of Peter. The building is of interest, because it must have looked very much like the church of the Ascension on the Mount of Olives (p. 74).

32 *right*. Inside the Church of the Primacy of Peter at Tabgha, on the Sea of Galilee. Here, Jesus said: 'Upon this Rock Peter I will build my Church.'

31 *opposite*. The Franciscan church on top of the Mount of Beatitudes, traditional site of the Sermon on the Mount, with the Sea of Galilee behind.

33 *right*. Steps from which the Apostles would have seen the Risen Christ as they mounted with their catch from the Sea of Galilee.

34 *below*. Tabgha, near the site of the Feeding of the Five Thousand.

35 *above*. Fifth-century mosaic of loaves and fishes in the Church of the Multiplication of Bread, the earliest surviving illustration of a gospel story.

Tabgha lies nearly three miles south-west of Capernaum, of which its abundant streams made it the industrial suburb, with mills, potteries and tanneries. The locality today contains two shrines. One is a little basalt chapel on the shore of the lake, to which stone steps lead down from the church. The fifth century pilgrim Aetheria says the steps were venerated as having borne the imprint of the feet of Jesus.

Two hundred yards south of this building stands the most interesting church of the whole region. The event here commemorated is the Multiplication of the Bread and Fishes (Matthew 13.13–21). A fifth century mosaic in the apse behind the main altar shows a basket containing four round loaves, each marked with a cross, flanked on either side by a local fish. It has lasted to our own day as the earliest known illustration of a Gospel story.

It is from Mount Tabor that we have our last view of Galilee, that sentinel which towers above the Plain of Esdraelon on its eastern side, 1843 feet above sea-level.

36 *over*. Lake Galilee from the Mount of the Beatitudes.

37. Mount Tabor, the traditional site of the Transfiguration of Jesus.

From its summit you may see most of Galilee and the land of Gilead beyond Jordan, as well as 'the glory of Carmel' above Megiddo. The mountain was renowned of old, equated with Hermon itself. 'The north and the south thou hast created them: Tabor and Hermon shall rejoice in thy name' (Psalm 89.12). In Christian tradition Tabor was accepted as the scene of the Transfiguration, described by all three of the Synoptic evangelists. The summit of the mountain, so often the scene of strife in former ages, now supports two churches, a small Orthodox one on the north side, and a very imposing one on the south side, belonging to the Franciscans, with a convent and hostel attached to it. From the windows of the hostel, you have an aerial view of Nain, of Endor, of Gideon's fountain, with Samaria and Judaea away to the south.

38. The Franciscan Church of the Transfiguration on Mount Tabor. The mosaic in the upper apse depicts Jesus transfigured, standing between Moses and Elijah.

The church itself was built in 1921 to 1924, and is one of Barluzzi's earliest masterpieces. The spacious colonnaded nave leads to an apse in two tiers; the axis of the church being east and west, the lower floor of the apse is reached by twelve steps down from the floor of the nave. It is in the form of an arched chapel. At the end of the apse is a window, decorated with two peacocks, traditional eastern symbols of immortality, and so contrived that the first rays of the rising sun shall shine through it, and, reflected from the gold and lapis-lazuli mosaics of the ceiling and walls, irradiate the whole chapel. The setting sun, shining through the great west window, illuminates the upper apse.

Galilee, Nazareth, Cana, Capernaum, Bethsaida, Tabor – all of them contribute to the eternal picture, a picture which knows neither past, nor present, nor future but is for ever.

43

39 *below.* Map of Jerusalem showing the Holy Sites.

40 *right.* Bethany, seen from the house of Martha and Mary.

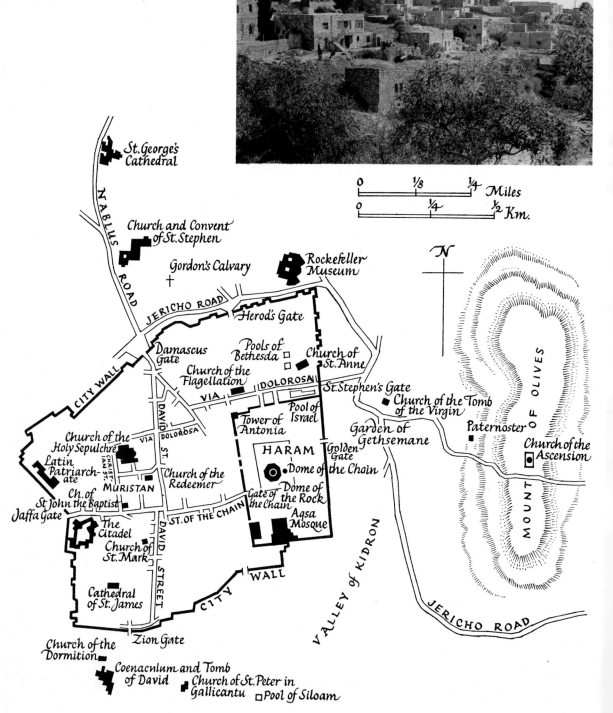

St. George's Cathedral

NABLUS ROAD

Church and Convent of St. Stephen

Gordon's Calvary

Rockefeller Museum

0   1/8   1/4 *Miles*
0   1/4   1/2 *Km.*

N

JERICHO ROAD

Herod's Gate

Damascus Gate

Pools of Bethesda

Church of St. Anne

Church of the Flagellation

VIA   DOLOROSA

St. Stephen's Gate

Church of the Tomb of the Virgin

CITY WALL

Church of the Holy Sepulchre

VIA DOLOROSA ST.

Latin Patriarch-ate

CHRISTIAN ST.

MURISTAN

DAVID ST.

Tower of Antonia

Pool of Israel

Garden of Gethsemane

Paternoster

MOUNT OF OLIVES

Church of the Ascension

HARAM

Golden Gate

Dome of the Chain

Church of the Redeemer

Ch. of St. John the Baptist

Jaffa Gate

Gate of the Chain

Dome of the Rock

Aqsa Mosque

ST. OF THE CHAIN

The Citadel

Church of St. Mark

DAVID STREET

VALLEY OF KIDRON

CITY WALL

Cathedral of St. James

JERICHO ROAD

Zion Gate

Church of the Dormition

Coenaculum and Tomb of David

Church of St. Peter in Gallicantu

Pool of Siloam

4 The Way of the Cross

So FAR as is known to us, Jesus after his boyhood never spent a night in Jerusalem, until the awful vigil before the Crucifixion. As was his custom, after his day's labour, teaching in the city, he sought rest; and this rest he found in the home of some friends of his, a brother and two sisters called Lazarus, Mary and Martha who lived at Bethany. Bethany lies rather less than two miles from Jerusalem. It is a charming village set in a horseshoe fold on the south-east flank of the Mount of Olives, the last habitable locality before the road plunges down through the wilderness to Jericho and the Jordan. Besides his three close friends, Jesus had another acquaintance in Bethany, a man called Simon, afflicted with leprosy. While they were all having supper in his house, Mary anointed Jesus with some very precious spice, an act which won great renown, both as prefiguring the embalming of Jesus' own body after the descent from the Cross, and also as setting a scale of values which rejected materialist standards.

The most famous of all Jesus' visits to Bethany occurred when he was in Transjordan (so John alone of the Evangelists tells us (ch. 11)), when a message was brought to him that Lazarus was very ill. After a deliberate delay of two days, Jesus decided to go back across the river, and up to Bethany. On arrival he was told that Lazarus was already dead and laid in his grave. John tells us that Jesus summoned Lazarus to leave his tomb and that Lazarus did so, having been in it for four days. The event created a great stir; and is represented by John to have been the final link in the chain of fear and resentment which made the orthodox hierarchy decide that Jesus must be eliminated, as otherwise 'the Romans' – only here mentioned as such in all the Gospels – 'shall come and take away both our place and nation'.

It was but natural that Bethany should very early become a focus of veneration, heightened by the fact that it was from Bethphage, a hamlet of Bethany 'where two ways meet' that the Triumphal Entry into Jerusalem took its way, an event annually celebrated over the same route on Palm Sunday.

41. The traditional Tomb of Lazarus at Bethany.

42. Palm Sunday procession from Bethphage to Jerusalem following the route which Jesus took.

The church at Bethany is austere, cold as a mausoleum, windowless like a grave, but so constructed that the light of heaven enters its dome from above – an allegory in stone such as Barluzzi habitually employed. A short distance to the west of the church stand the remains of a Crusader tower. This is the sole relic of a great monastery, later a convent, built by the Franks in honour of Mary and Martha.

From Bethphage, where again a mediaeval church has been incorporated in a more recent one, the way led beneath 'the

43. The Lion or St Stephen's Gate as it now is.

purple brows of Olivet' down towards Gethsemane. There are several paths from the summit of the Mount to the Garden of Gethsemane. Of the convents which crown the ridge it will be more appropriate to speak in a later context; but between them and the Garden there is a shrine in a garth belonging to the Franciscans known as *Dominus Flevit*, 'The Lord Wept', because it was here that, according to a very old tradition, 'when he was come near he beheld the city and wept over it, saying, if thou hadst known, even thou, at least in this thy day, the things which belong to thy peace! but now they are hid from thine eyes' (Luke 19.41).

46 *opposite*. Garden of Gethsemane. These ancient olive trees are descendants of those which sheltered Jesus and his disciples on the night before Good Friday.

The Garden itself contains two great churches. The upper one is Russian. It was built by the Czar Alexander III in 1888. The lower church is by far better known. Again it is Franciscan, and is built in such a manner that it covers the traditional rock of a very early church. At several places on the floor portions of the original mosaics may still be seen.

Most beautiful of all in Gethsemane is the garden itself, 'for Jesus oft times resorted thither with his disciples' (John 18.2). Here beneath these most ancient olive trees – Gethsemane means 'oil-press' – sprung perhaps from the roots of the very trees which sheltered Jesus and his friends, you have a feeling of communion with them which very few other places can convey.

We too now enter Jerusalem, the Holy City. The entire town is a Holy Place.

44 *above*. Jerusalem from the Church of Dominus Flevit (the Lord wept) where Jesus wept over Jerusalem during his triumphal entry.

45 *right*. The Mount of Olives seen from Jerusalem. On the left, the Church of All Nations in the Garden of Gethsemane and to the right the Russian Church of Saint Mary Magdalene.

47 *opposite*. The Pool of Bethesda where Jesus told the sick man: 'Take up thy bed and walk'; and the Church of Saint Anne.

Just outside St Stephen's Gate is a pool known as the pool of Our Lady Mary, and just inside is the church of St Anne. Again, we have a church built over a crypt, which in this case is venerated as the home of Mary's parents, Joachim and Anna. This church is one of the most beautiful in all Jerusalem, and has recently been restored to its original dignified austerity, although it was badly damaged in the 1967 war. The style is Burgundian Romanesque, and the building was erected in the middle of the twelfth century by the queen of king Baldwin I who liberally endowed it. It was the conventual church of the Benedictine nun Yvette, sister of Queen Melisende. The church owes its preservation to Saladin, who transformed it into a Muslim college, later to become a mosque.

48 *below*. The Cenacle or Room of the Last Supper on Mount Zion, reconstructed by the Crusaders. In the corner is a Muslim shrine.

Claimant for the status of Upper Room is the little Church of St Mark, not far from the Armenian cathedral.

49 *above*. 'Game of the King' paving stone which the Roman soldiers may have used to gamble for the condemned man's garments.

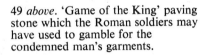

50 *above right*. The Roman pavement found beneath the Convent of the Ladies of Zion believed to be part of the Gabbatha on which Jesus stood before Pilate.

51 *opposite*. The interior of the Syrian Orthodox Church of Saint Mark.

It is the traditional house of Mark, and the headquarters of the Syrian Orthodox bishopric of Jerusalem. The rite of this Church is a Syriac form of the ancient rite of Antioch, attributed to James, brother of Jesus. The Syriac language which is used in their liturgy is a form of Aramaic. This was the language spoken by Jesus and his disciples, and it is still the vernacular of certain villages near Damascus.

The road from St Anne rises steadily towards a large level platform. It was on this great podium that the Tower of Antonia stood. It was a vast square building, with a frontage towards the southern or Temple front of 375 feet, almost exactly the same as that of Buckingham Palace. So huge was this fortress that its site now houses a school (from which the Good Friday procession starts), the Convent of the Flagellation, with yet another of Barluzzi's chapels, and the Convent of the Dames de Zion, whose own chapel incorporates a portion of Hadrian's arch, of which the central vault here spans the street. The Ladies have brought to light in the basement of their convent a pavement, or Gabbatha, which is by many believed to be the very one mentioned in John 19.13, as the scene of Pilate's judgement of Jesus, the very Praetorium of Mark 15.16.

By the end of the fourth century, as we know from Aetheria, it was held that the Praetorium was here or hereabouts, and so it is natural that the 'Way of the Cross' should start from here. The fourteen Stations of the Cross, as now denoted in Jerusalem on the Via Dolorosa, and as represented on the walls of churches in all parts of the world are, like so much in Jerusalem, a harmony of East and West. Aetheria tells us that on the evening of Maundy Thursday pilgrims went down to Gethsemane, and thence set out for

53 *opposite*. Rock cut prison cells below Saint Peter in Gallicantu where Jesus may have been held.

Golgotha during the night, so as to arrive at dawn on Good Friday in the atrium of Calvary, where the reading of the Gospel describing the trial in the Praetorium ended the procession. Aetheria therefore must have passed along much of the present Via Dolorosa.

In the eighth century another route was followed, which led up through the southern part of the city to St Peter in Gallicantu and the House of Caiaphas. During the eleventh century public Christian processions were forbidden, and the sites connected with the Way of the Cross were commemorated in the Church of the Holy Sepulchre, in the chapels which still bear those ascriptions. Under the Crusaders, both the 'southern' and the 'northern' (existing) way were in vogue, and the patriarch declined to prescribe one as being more authentic than the other. It was in the fourteenth century that the Franciscans began to organize the Way as a devotional exercise; and in the next century an Oxford don who made his pilgrimage uses for the first time the word 'stations' in connection with it. The word came into general use in the next century.

52 *below*. Saint Peter in Gallicantu or 'of the cock crowing', built on the traditional site of the House of Caiaphas where the first trial of Jesus took place.

54 *above*. Good Friday. Pilgrims and priests of the Orthodox Church arrive at the Church of the Holy Sepulchre.

55 *above right*. Via Dolorosa, the Way of the Cross along which Jesus walked from his judgement to his crucifixion. Along this are now arranged the Stations of the Cross.

The Turks often prevented pilgrims from making their corporate devotions along the Way, and so returned pilgrims started to reproduce it in their own countries, using pictures or sculptures of the various sites commemorated. Alvary of Cordova, who died in 1420, was one of the first to do so: in 1491 a nun of Messina did much the same. Pilgrims would make notes and take measurements to ensure that their own Ways would be as accurate as possible. Nuremberg had its Way in 1472, Louvain in 1505. This last contained seven stations, and became the model for our existing one. In 1563 Pascha of Louvain (who had never been in Jerusalem) published his *Peregrination spirituelle*, which notes fourteen stations. This work and another like it which followed in 1584 had a profound influence, which caused the tide of devotion to turn back to Jerusalem, and made men to seek in the Holy City itself that with which they had grown familiar in their own countries.

Thus the present Via Dolorosa came into being. The term was in use in 1550; in the following century it assumed almost the form in which we now know it, which was finally crystallized in 1855.

56. Topography and site of Calvary.

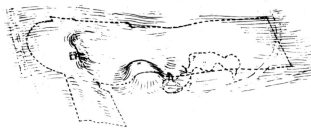

The later excavations on the site of the Church.

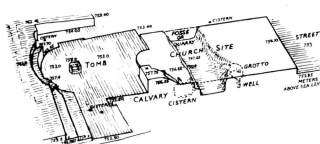

The Basilica of Constantine.

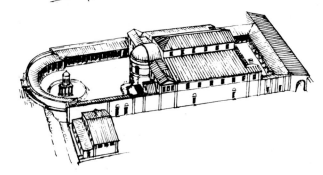

The completed Church with Rotunda.

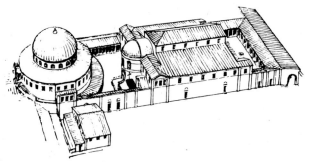

5 The Holy Sepulchre

FOR MORE than sixteen hundred years the church of the
Holy Sepulchre, or of the Resurrection as it is locally known,
has been the most revered of Holy Places. Like the church
of the Nativity at Bethlehem it has survived since the very
earliest days of the Christian·Roman empire; but unlike that
shrine it has been altered and destroyed and rebuilt so often
that the original plan is only in our own days being once
more clarified.

To start with, the site itself may puzzle the pilgrim; but
in fact it could not be better authenticated both by Scripture
and by modern archaeology. The three synoptic Gospels all
say that Joseph of Arimathaea, a leading Jewish councillor,
obtained permission from Pilate to bury Jesus in a tomb he
had just had made for himself. John adds the vital detail
that this tomb was in a garden. Just as St Martin's church
in Trafalgar Square was once 'in the fields' so this quarter
of Jerusalem was outside the city walls in the time of Jesus.

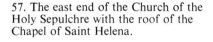

57. The east end of the Church of the
Holy Sepulchre with the roof of the
Chapel of Saint Helena.

ΝΗΕΠΙΤΟΝΑΙΤΗΕ ΣΙΕΜΙ
ΗΑ ΓΝΕ ΤΙ
ΗΑΓΙΑΠΤΟΛΙϹΙΕΡΟΥϹΑ
ΛΗΡ

ΙΝ

ΕΤΑΡ

ΤΟΕΝΝΑ
ΒΕΘΩΦΟ
ΕΡΧΤΑ
ΘΑΜΝΑ
ΑΚΕΛ
ΔΑΜΑ

59 *above*. The Madaba Map, the sixth-century mosaic in the church at Madaba, Jordan, showing Jerusalem as rebuilt by Hadrian and embellished by Constantine. Held upside down it shows in the middle of the upper colonnaded street the Basilica of Constantine with its triple entrance (the original church on this site). Beyond it is the Tomb Rotunda, and on the left is the open piazza of Calvary (marked by a cross).

58 *opposite*. The domes of the Church of the Holy Sepulchre from the tower of the Lutheran Church.

But how was the tomb situated 'in a garden' and at the same time so near the gate that it was adjacent to the place of execution? The answer is that the richer a man was – and Joseph was rich – the nearer to the gate would his tomb be situated. To this day the Muslim cemetery outside St Stephen's Gate illustrates this rule.

After quelling the second Jewish revolt in AD 135 the emperor Hadrian razed Jerusalem, and laid out on its ruins a new Roman town called Aelia Capitolina. Special care was taken to obliterate Jewish or Judaeo-Christian shrines. The Sepulchre which Christians were already venerating was therefore desecrated and replaced by a temple of Venus, patroness of Rome, just as the Grotto at Bethlehem was dedicated to Adonis. When in 326 the empress Helena, mother of Constantine the first Christian emperor, came to Jerusalem to build churches over the principal sites connected with the life and ministry of Jesus, it was easy for the bishop to point to the temple and to explain its origin.

Having thus recovered the site, what did the bishop and the empress put on it? For this we have unique concrete evidence: two mosaics. One is what is known as the 'Madaba mosaic' on the floor of a church in Transjordan which shows Jerusalem as it was in the sixth century, that is to say the Aelia Capitolina of Hadrian. From the *cardo maximus* or main street five broad steps on the west side lead up to a triple portal. Behind this there is a building on an east-west axis with a pitched roof, and behind that a circular domed building. To the south there is a raised area, separate from the two buildings.

Thus we see that the first church consisted not of one building but of two, with a detached area between them, the whole surrounded with a wall ending at the west end in an apse with three *exedrae*, or semi-circular wings, so that its plan looked like a clover-leaf, the symbol of the Trinity.

We now turn to the mosaic in the apse of the church of Santa Pudenziana in Rome. This was first designed two hundred years earlier than the Madeba map, and it shows exactly the same plan, only in greater detail, and as seen from the south. The triple portal, the basilica with the pitched roof, the circular domed building, the forecourt building, all are there. And in the foreground, in the open, is Calvary (Latin: *calvaria*, bald-head, i.e. Golgotha, 'place of a skull') surmounted by the Cross. The testimony of these two mosaics exactly tallies with the literary description given by Eusebius, the Palestinian historian who was the friend of Constantine, and by a pilgrim from Bordeaux who was in Jerusalem in 333.

It was the circular domed building that housed the Sepulchre itself. In order to provide a circular processional way around it, the rock-hewn tomb was separated from the hill out of which it had been carved, so as to be free-standing. It was treated just as the Hellenistic tombs in the Kedron valley were, the so-called Absalom's pillar and tomb of Zachariah. At the same time and for the same reason the rock of Calvary was similarly cut back.

This triple complex of shrines – basilica (known as the *martyrion*, or place of witness), 'garden' and rotunda – experienced many vicissitudes. It was wrecked by the Persians in 614, rebuilt, destroyed by Hakim in 1010, and only partially restored in 1048. The *martyrion* had gone for ever.

The Crusaders, passionate builders as they were, replaced the lost *martyrion* with a Romanesque cathedral – a very fine one indeed, with, as we can now again see, a rib-vaulted roof, the earliest of its kind after that of Durham cathedral (1092). The crossing is crowned with a splendid dome. The Tomb was given a new dome, too.

60 *opposite*. 'Church of the Holy Sepulchre and Dome of the Rock, Jerusalem', from The Book of Hours of René d'Anjou, 1436 (Egerton MS 1070, f5).

The Crusaders re-roofed the crypt, St Helena's chapel as it is known, and took in Calvary and the 'garden' east of the rotunda. Thus for the first time, although the church was much smaller in area than as originally built, Calvary, the Tomb, the 'garden' and the basilica were all grouped under one roof.

Gradually the whole glorious fabric fell into decay. In 1808 a fire ravaged it, and in 1810 the building was hastily botched up. In 1927 an earthquake, the latest of at least fifteen, nearly brought it to the ground. A new dawn arose in 1959, when the three major occupants of the church, Orthodox, Armenian and Latin, agreed on a comprehensive restoration. The work was placed under the general direction of a Dominican architect-priest, Father Charles Couasnon. Already much of the ancient splendour, and light, had been restored. The Crusader cathedral is almost wholly renewed. Where original work has disappeared, it has been skilfully supplied by modern craftsmen. One such new capital on the north side commemorates the visit of the Pope in 1964.

The restoration work has not only revealed the beauty of the mediaeval shrine, it has also shown that far more exists of the Constantinian original than was previously supposed.

Let us now enter the building through the door in the southern façade, which has been restored and consolidated so that we can once again behold it as it was when the Crusaders built it in the twelfth century. The double doorway, of which only the left-hand door is now in use, bore lintels with sculptures on them, one of foliage and the other representing the raising of Lazarus with the onlookers holding their noses. These are now in the Palestine Museum. They were carved locally, as incised patterns on their backs have shown. The marble doorposts are starred with little crosses and an occasional name and date, souvenirs of pilgrims of long ago. On our right as we enter, Calvary rises sheer from the ground 'about the height of a lance' as the Crusaders reckoned it, and supports two chapels, one Orthodox and one Latin. The living rock in this the very place of Crucifixion is clearly visible both at the top and in the Chapel of Adam at the base.

Descending from Calvary, we turn west and pass the Stone of the anointing. This commemorates the anointing of the body of Jesus by Joseph and Nicodemus as recorded in John 19.39. In view of the hurried and secret nature of the burial the anointing must have been done between Calvary and the Sepulchre. To this we now turn: it is only a few paces away, in the aedicule (as it is known) in the middle of the Rotunda.

61. The Chapel of Calvary on top of the rock which stands up perpendicularly 'the height of a lance' from the ground. On the left is the Orthodox Chapel, centre the Armenian Altar and right the Latin Chapel.

Komnenos of Mitylene, the architect responsible for the 1810 reconstruction had to work very quickly, lest some other religious body, despite Europe's preoccupation with Napoleon, might wheedle the Porte into rescinding in their own favour the permissive *firman*. Komnenos had to use whatever means came to hand to keep the structure from collapse, which in the days before concrete and steel meant masses of stone and plaster. So it came about that the calcined survivors of the original delicate columns were encased in square splints; windows were blocked up and supporting walls hastily constructed. Some of these last two blemishes have already been removed. It is known that within the piers some at least of the columns still exist, and that with the aid of modern stainless steel pins, it may be possible to reveal them once again.

The aedicule itself, which covers the actual tomb, must soon be renewed, as it is no longer stable. Before the actual Sepulchre there is an antechamber, a fairly modern addition, because the old engravings, mosaics and ivories represent the Tomb as a single cell. Vestiges of it were still there in 1809, and were again descried in 1927, when the marble slab within was repaired after the earthquake. (Here, as on Calvary, it had been necessary to cover the original rock with marble, to prevent the pious depredations of pilgrims.)

In addition to the 'Big Three' communities, Orthodox, Armenian and Latin, two other Churches have visible status in the building. At the back of the Tomb there is a little shrine belonging to the Copts, that is the national Church of Egypt, who have a cathedral and convent near the ancient portal. They have been here since 1573, their status having been consolidated by the Egyptian viceroy Mehmet Ali (1832–40). Their liturgy follows either the rite of St Cyril of Alexandria or those of the Greek Fathers, St Gregory and St Basil.

The fifth Church to worship within the Church is that of the Syrians, whom we have already met in the House of Mark. Their tiny chapel, which is actually Armenian property, is just across the ambulatory from that of the Copts, in what was the central exedra of Constantine's complex. The Ethiopians (Abyssinians) formerly possessed rights within the church, and, relegated to the roof of St Helena's chapel, still maintain their presence.

Hard by the Syrian chapel are two tombs. They are small and dim, and were partly cut away when the Rotunda was formed. They are of great value as evidence that the area where we are standing was outside the walls when the burials took place, for burial within them was forbidden.

62 *opposite*. The Stone of the Anointing where the body of Jesus was anointed as it was brought down from Calvary to be placed in the adjacent tomb of Joseph of Arimathaea.

64 *above*. The entrance to the Tomb from the Chapel of Calvary.

63 *opposite*. Inside the Tomb showing, in the foreground, the stone on which Our Lord's body rested.

On the north side of the Rotunda several interesting features await us. Passing through the arch which leads to the Franciscan church, we enter a passage at the end of which in 1959–61 some impressive pillars and arches of the church as restored by Monomachus, the Byzantine emperor, in 1048, have come to light. We can also see the remnant of the actual staircase by which Crusader patriarchs entered the church from their palace in Christian Street, where the blocked-up portal is still there. Between this structure and the Rotunda the exploration of 1962 uncovered part of the original northern exedra.

We may now investigate the eastern portion of the church. The main part of this is occupied by the renovated Crusader church, now the Orthodox cathedral or *Katholikon* as it is styled. Following the ambulatory round, we pass on the north side some very old Byzantine pillars re-used by the Crusaders. Behind the apse of the Katholikon we come to four commemorative chapels, the Prison of Christ, and the chapels of St Longinus, the Division of Vestments and the Derision. Between the last two is a sloping staircase leading down to the chapel of St Helena, the original crypt. From

65 *above*. Crosses cut into the walls of the church by mediaeval pilgrims—perhaps Chaucer's Wyfe of Bath was one of them—to celebrate the consummation of their pilgrimage.

it another thirteen steps bring us to the Chapel of the Finding of the Cross. It looks as though it had once been a cistern, which later became, as so many old cisterns do, a repository for unwanted things. The tradition, later to become of such vast import, that it was here that St Helena identified the True Cross, is first mentioned by St Ambrose in 395. The chapel used to belong to the Georgians, but is now served by the Orthodox and Latins. The left-hand altar was given by the Archduke Maximilian of Austria, who later became emperor of Mexico, where he was assassinated in 1864.

Again on the sidewalls of the staircase which leads us back to the ambulatory are scores of little crosses, memorials of unknown pilgrims who had braved so much danger, endured so much hardship, to visit what was for them the holiest place on earth, the very gate of heaven itself. This church, in its vicissitudes, its changes and chances, spoliations and renewals has for sixteen hundred years been the mirror of human life itself. It is the most human church on earth, but in its essence and origin it is also the most divine, this church of the Resurrection.

66 *opposite*. The little Coptic chapel at the rear of the Tomb.

70

6 'First Fruits of the Spirit'

68 *above*. The Mount of Olives from Jerusalem looking towards the Church of the Ascension.

THE RESURRECTION was an accepted fact within twenty-four hours. Everyone had been on edge in Jerusalem that morning. The earthquake which two days earlier had shaken the Temple and created the three-hour-long dust-storm (Matthew 27, Mark 15, Luke 23) had been followed as earthquakes often are by another seismic shock (Matthew 28.2), during which the circular stone had been rolled away from the Sepulchre. When the women first brought their story of the empty tomb, it was dismissed as 'idle tales', even though Mary of Magdala declared that she had talked with the Lord, who had forbidden her to touch him.

By the evening doubt had been dispelled: male testimony had in the end overcome uncertainty. Two of Jesus' companions had been bound for Emmaus, one of them Cleopas, a member of Jesus' inner circle. Jesus had appeared to them 'in the breaking of bread'. Hastening back to Jerusalem (the double journey has been proved to be feasible), they found the eleven apostles and told them their news. This was at once validated by the appearance of the Risen Lord. All doubt was now at an end. The Resurrection was a fact, and the story of Christianity as a Faith had begun. A band of frightened and fleeing peasants had been transformed at one moment of time into a group of bold and convinced confessors. That was the abiding miracle which started the Christian Faith. The Christian Church was yet to be.

Forty days was the period which the disciples reckoned between the first and last appearances of the Risen Lord. On the fortieth morning Jesus was removed from the sight of his followers. The traditional setting of the Ascension is on the summit of the Mount of Olives.

The Mount of Olives is yet another proof that the Gospel story is best comprehended not in buildings made with hands. True, there were shrines here from very early times, one being the magnificent church of the Eleona erected by the empress Helena; but it is the mountain-ridge itself which is the epicentre of the grand panorama of time, space and eternity which the summit commands.

The seal was set upon the apostles' mission at the feast of Pentecost following the fateful Passover. Pentecost is Greek for the fiftieth, the Jewish feast of harvest.

67 *opposite*. The old Roman paved way at El-Qubeiheh along which, perhaps, Jesus walked with the two travellers after his resurrection. This is not the only claimant to be the ancient Emmaus (see 125 *below*).

73

69 *above*. The Golden or Beautiful Gate by which the Apostles used to enter in the Temple after the Ascension.

70 *above right*. The Church of the Ascension at the top of the Mount of Olives; originally it was open to the sky.

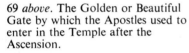

71 *opposite*. The Armenian Cathedral of Saint James, built on the site of the room where tongues of fire descended on the Apostles at the first Pentecost.

On this occasion the followers of Jesus experienced a spiritual renewal so dynamic that it caused a great stir. The spiritual experience was accompanied by a physical disturbance such as the onset of the raging Sirocco often produces, with some form of electrical storm, which in Jerusalem can be highly spectacular and alarming. Visitors of at least fifteen nationalities were present at the Feast. In the excitement which made some of the company seem intoxicated – as they were, but not with wine – some of the utterances may well have sounded like gibberish; but for the comprehension of their message not fifteen tongues were necessary but only two, Aramaic and Greek, of which everybody present knew one, and many both.

The apostles (as they now were in truth), at once set out on their missions. In Jerusalem the head of the new community was Jacob, or James, brother of Jesus. He, together with James son of Zebedee, is commemorated in the great Armenian cathedral near the Citadel. This building, architecturally distinguished and richly ornamented, appears to stand on the site of the great 'Upper Church' shown on the Madeba map. This was the mother church of Jerusalem.

Peter and John continued to frequent the Temple where they had so often listened to their Master. Here they healed a lame man, over forty years of age. This cure attracted much attention, and a large crowd soon collected. Large crowds always arouse apprehension in Jerusalem, and so the Sadducees in whose charge the Temple was, with their chief of police, came and arrested Peter and John. They escaped from prison.

COLLEGE LIBRARY
COLLEGE OF TECHNOLOGY
CARNARVON ROAD
SOUTHEND-ON-SEA, ESSEX

72 *opposite*. 'The Stoning of Stephen' by Beato Angelico (Vatican Museum, Rome).

A well-to-do, fiery young man from the great city of Tarsus in Cilicia, named Saul, determined on direct action. Saul chose as his target a youth called Stephen, who held a junior office in the new sect, that of *diakonos*, deacon or servitor. Saul accused him of blasphemy, a vague but lethal charge. At last the court had a victim. Stephen was condemned, dragged out of the city by the nearest gate, that is the northern one, and there on a little mound they stoned him to death. Saul directed the stoning-party and himself took charge of its clothes.

In the year 460 the Byzantine empress Eudokia built a basilica here to the memory of Stephen, the first Christian martyr. In 1882 the French Dominicans acquired the site, and after clearing it were able to incorporate in their new church, consecrated in 1900, vestiges of the original basilica. It now houses the world-famous Ecole Biblique et Archéologique.

73 *right*. The Damascus Gate by which Stephen, the first Christian martyr, was stoned to death.

A colleague of Stephen's, another deacon called Philip, showed an undaunted initiative in promoting the new society. He boldly went off to Samaria, where he spread the tidings with great success: the Samaritans had not forgotten the visit of Jesus himself and his conversation with that woman at the well of Sychar. Philip then went south. On the high road between Bethlehem and Hebron he fell in with an Ethiopian diplomatist, a royal treasurer, who was already attracted to Judaism, had been to Jerusalem to worship, and was reading the book of Isaiah as he drove along. Him too Philip convinced, and baptized at a spring – it is the only one so situated – on the left-hand side of the road a few miles beyond 'Arrub, with a Roman milestone lying near it. Philip then went on to Ashdod, and up to Caesarea, the Roman capital, where he lived.

Paul, as Saul was soon to become, is generally and rightly known as the apostle to the Gentiles; but the honour of being the first to bring Gentiles into the new society must be awarded to Philip the Deacon, who later on would be Paul's host in Caesarea itself.

Saul having gone off to Damascus bent on slaughter and arrest, the followers of Jesus in Jerusalem were able to breathe more freely. Thus Peter was led to go down to

76 right. A street near the site of
Simon the Tanner's house.

74 opposite above. The old town of
Jaffa (Joppa) where Saint Peter
dwelt with Simon the Tanner and
raised Tabitha from the dead. It was
from here that he was summoned to
Caesarea by the Roman officer
Cornelius who became the first
Gentile convert.

75 opposite below. The wayside well
on the road to Hebron where Saint
Philip baptized the Ethiopian treasurer.

Joppa. He passed through Lydda, and there cured a man
who had been bed-ridden for eight years. At Joppa he raised
Tabitha from her death-bed. He was staying with a tanner
called Simon, who carried on business close to the shore, so
that the effluent from his tannery could be channelled into
the sea. A Roman officer of the cohort called *Italica*,
stationed at Caesarea, hearing of Peter's arrival and remarkable activities, sent three soldiers to Simon's house to
bring Peter to Caesarea. When, after much heart-searching,
he arrived there he found Cornelius ripe for conversion to
the New Way, and baptized him into it.

The apostolic mission to Joppa was therefore worthy of
the most solemn commemoration. Just when the first
church arose here we do not know. But St Louis himself in
1248 founded within his newly fortified citadel a fine church
with twelve altars and confided it to the care of the Franciscans. Expelled with the Crusaders, the ever-tenacious
Franciscans were back in 1520. In 1654, they were there to
stay. The present church was inaugurated in 1891.

The traditional site of Simon the Tanner's house on the
sea-front is marked by a little mosque, now disused, below
the church. The raising of Tabitha is annually celebrated by
the Orthodox in the courtyard of the Russian church.

7 Paul: the Apostle to the Gentiles

77 *opposite*. Saint Paul depicted in the sixth-century mosaic in the Arian Baptistry at Ravenna.

78 *below*. The Cilician Gates on the road to Antioch through which Paul passed after parting from Barnabas at the outset of his second missionary journey.

JUST WHAT happened to Saul on that journey to Damascus we cannot tell, any more than we can tell what happened to St Augustine, or to St Ignatius Loyola, or to John Wesley or to General William Booth of the Salvation Army. What we do know is that, in a flash, the impeccably orthodox, militant Pharisee Saul was transformed into Paul the apostle.

For seventeen years after his conversion Paul and his new mission were in abeyance, dormant. Paul departed into Arabia, for a season of meditation. After going back to Damascus he visited Peter and Jacob (James) three years later in Jerusalem. He stayed only a fortnight, and then went back to his native Cilicia.

79 *above*. The first Christian Church
dedicated to Saint Peter at Antioch.

80 *right*. The altar in Saint Peter's
Church, Antioch.

81 *above*. The Byzantine Monastery of Saint Barnabas in Cyprus. It was Barnabas, a Cypriot, who took Paul on his first missionary journey.

82 *above right*. The tomb of Saint Barnabas in the Monastery.

Antioch, the great Syrian metropolis was the nearest international centre to Cilicia. It is only a hundred miles from Tarsus, and it was here that, secure from harassment by resentful Sadducees, the nascent community of the followers of the Master were first called Christians, that is were reckoned as members of a new, distinct society. A number of Greeks had now been brought into the fold, many of them by the enterprising labours of Barnabas, a Hellenistic Jew, a Levite, from Cyprus. Barnabas now recruited Paul; and the two of them set out on what is known as Paul's First Missionary Journey. There were to be three of them altogether, covering a period of some thirteen years followed by a journey from Jerusalem to Rome in the year AD 60.

During these peregrinations Paul established more Holy Places than any other apostle, disciple or saint in any epoch.

The first goal of the missionaries was Cyprus, the homeland of Barnabas, who at the outset of the tour was the leader. He is still commemorated by the monastery of St Barnabas, near Salamis, where they landed.

84 *opposite*. The Via Egnatia between Philippi and Kavalla. This great trunk road united the Adriatic and Byzantium which Paul travelled on his way to Thessalonika and Corinth.

83 *below*. Lake Egridir, south of Antioch in Pisidia, through which Saint Paul passed on his first journey.

The travellers then crossed over into Asia, passing through Perga, where magnificent ruins of the grand buildings which they beheld still stand, and ascended to another Antioch, that of Pisidia, and so made their way to Iconium, now Konya. Then by way of Lystra and Derbe they returned to Perga, and so at Attalia (Antalya), the picturesque port of Pamphylia, where they took ship for Antioch. They had been away for five years.

Paul now saw clearly that Europe must be his goal, and so down to Troas he went and proceeded thence to Philippi, named after the father of Alexander the Great. Philippi is the first Holy Place of Christendom in Europe.

Paul's advent in Greece has animated and inspired the Eastern Church from that day to this. In Thessalonica, in Athens, in Corinth, Paul planted the seeds of the Faith.

This second tour had lasted some four years and like the first it ended in Antioch.

85 *opposite*. The theatre, Miletus. It was in Miletus that Paul bade his sorrowful farewell to his friends from Ephesus. It was his final utterance in Asia.

86 *below*. Ephesus. The marble way which led originally from the harbour to the city. In front lies the great theatre in which the riot of the silversmiths, concerned about the effectiveness of Saint Paul's preaching, took place.

Paul's third tour was designed to be one of confirmation and corroboration of already existing churches, as we may now begin to call them. The Galatian centres were visited for a third time, so were Philippi and Corinth, Troas, too, with this time Assos and Mitylene. The tour produced nothing so radically innovating for history and mankind as the second, but it did result in Luke's giving us the most intimate picture we have of what life in the Roman empire was like. Paul had touched at Ephesus on his second journey, but now on his third he stayed there for three years. His sojourn was full of incident, culminating in the first trade union riot on record. The whole story is related in great and subtly humorous detail in Acts 19.

Tyre in Syria was Paul's port of re-entry to the Levant. From Tyre to Ptolemais, or Acre as it is known to us, from its Crusader associations, Paul went on to Caesarea, the Roman capital.

87 *right*. Tyre, shrine and view over the harbour at sunrise. Paul spent seven days here with his faithful adherents on his courageous last visit to Jerusalem.

88 *below*. Rome, the Eternal City, with the River Tiber in the foreground. On the right is the Castel Sant' Angelo, originally built as a mausoleum for himself by the Emperor Hadrian, who had sought to obliterate the tomb of Jesus in Jerusalem; and on the left, triumphant, is the dome of Saint Peter's Basilica in the Vatican.

That Paul was determined to see Rome we already know; but it is doubtful whether he foresaw what was to be the manner of his going there. From Caesarea he had once again visited Jerusalem, bearing alms collected for the poorer brethren during his recent tour, and in order to prove his orthodoxy had undertaken to pay the expenses of four Nazirites who were desirous of discharging their holy vows (see Numbers 6). Unfortunately on the seventh and last day of these pious exercises, Paul was recognized by some of his old opponents from Asian Jewry. They set upon him and instigated a riot, calling Paul a blasphemer and a polluter of the Temple. Paul was mobbed and was taken into protective custody by the Roman commandant of the Antonia, despite his bold and eloquent apologia, delivered in Hebrew from the steps of the fortress to the bloodthirsty throng below.

89 below right. Caesarea. Ruins of the ancient harbour built by Herod the Great. It was from Caesarea, then the capital of the Roman province of Judaea, that Paul set out on his last journey, which led him to Rome.

The commandant sent Paul down to Caesarea. There he was detained quite illegally for two years by the governor, an ex-slave of the imperial household called Felix. Finally Paul, having appealed to Caesar, as he was entitled to, was sent to Rome by Felix's successor, Festus. Luke who was with Paul used these two years profitably to collect the eye-witness accounts on which, as he tells us at its outset, his Gospel was to be based.

Before Paul reached Rome, accompanied by Luke, yet one more, final, occasion was to be made immortal by Luke's graphic pen, namely that of the most famous and most successful shipwreck in history.

It happened off the east coast of Malta. We can still visit the little sandy cove in what is now St Paul's Bay where the crew, the guards and the prisoners all came safe to shore. It is called in Maltese *mistra*, that is refuge, to this day.

In the spring of AD 61 the party set out in safety, and soon reached Italy.

For two years Paul lived in his own rented house in Rome, enjoying comparative freedom. We do not know the year of Paul's death; but since the 'two years' just mentioned would bring us to the threshold of the year AD 64, in which Nero tried to shift the guilt for the great fire of that year onto the Christians, it is not unreasonable to suppose that Paul, so prominent a member of the Christian community, was among the many who perished. Some were torn to pieces by wild beasts, others used as human torches to illuminate Nero's Vatican gardens. Paul, being a Roman citizen, would be exempt from such revolting barbarity. He was to be executed outside the Walls in accordance with Roman custom. The place of his execution is attested by early and constant tradition. He was led out of the City by the Porta Trigemina, past the Pyramid of Cestius at the foot of which John Keats lies buried. The procession turned into the Ostian Way, where the basilica of St Paul-without-the-Walls now stands, then diverged onto the Laurentian Way. At the third milestone they reached the Salvian Marsh, where today is the Trappist monastery of *Tre Fontane*, 'Three Springs'. This monastery is the oldest in Rome, having been founded by Pope Honorius I (625–40). It lies in a little dell. There are three shrines within the precincts, one of which shelters the Three Fountains.

Here Paul was beheaded. He was buried nearer Rome where the basilica of St Paul-without-the-Walls now stands. The church as we now see it is a reconstruction after a disastrous fire in 1823. It still seems to be imbued with some of the personality of Paul himself, its depths, its darknesses, its disasters, above all its vanquishing strength and triumph.

91 *top*. The Basilica of Saint Paul-without-the-Walls in Rome, seen from the west.

92 *above*. Relief of Saint Paul's severed head at the shrine of Tre Fontane, the three fountains, which commemorates the place of Saint Paul's execution.

90 *opposite*. Malta. The place between two seas where Paul's ship was wrecked in AD 60. The statue of Saint Paul can just be discerned on the left-hand edge of the peninsula.

8 Caesars and Saints

THE STRUGGLE for the soul of Rome was to be bitter and long drawn out. The battle between Caesars and Saints lasted for two and a half centuries, from the advent of Paul in AD 61, until the establishment of Constantine as sole emperor and first Christian ruler of Rome in 312.

In view of the predominant role that Rome was to play and still fills in the history of Christendom, it is natural that the development of Christian Rome should be central to any consideration of Christian history and topography. But it would be wrong to dwell on Rome only. In fact the Faith spread very rapidly and widely to other parts of the world, even beyond the bounds of the Roman empire, long before Rome itself became the centre of Christendom.

Of Rome it might be said that the whole city is a Holy Place and so in a sense it is; but that it ever became so is one of the miracles of history. The first Roman emperor to recognize Christians as such was Nero, whose onslaught upon the nascent Church gave it independent status. A 'kingdom not of this world' – what an utterly anarchistic idea. Had not Virgil himself, the noblest Roman of them all, proclaimed Rome's destiny to be the ruler of this world? Anyone who dared to controvert that claim must be crushed in the name of law and order.

When you have two political and moral systems so utterly opposed to each other, each competing for the direction of the brief and transitory life of humanity, a clash is inevitable. During the first two centuries of the Roman empire the struggle swayed now in one direction and now in the other. It was only towards the middle of the following century that organized and general persecutions, as opposed to sporadic and local outbreaks, took place. About the beginning of the year 250 an imperial edict ordered all citizens to perform a pagan sacrifice in the presence of special commissioners, who would issue official certificates of conformity. (Examples of such certificates have survived on Egyptian papyrus.) There were many lapses; but the steadfastness of the majority greatly fortified the Christian Church. The bishops of Rome, Jerusalem and Antioch were

93 The Church of the Tomb of the Virgin in Jerusalem, of which only the doorway and crypt remain. The church was destroyed by the Persians in 614 and again by the Saracens in 1187.

killed, the great Origen was arrested. Eight years later St Cyprian of Carthage was condemned to death and made a noble end, even rewarding his executioner for his trouble, in the city where half a century earlier Felicity and Perpetua had met death with such fortitude. All three of these martyrs are commemorated at Carthage by the foundations of the basilicas which were raised in their honour. The last official attempt to eradicate Christianity in the empire occurred under Diocletian, and his evil counsellor Galerius. Four successive edicts were issued to that end; until in 311 the unbelievable occurred: Galerius himself recanted. Next year a young man arrived from York, where he had been hailed as emperor by his troops. His name was Constantine, and he was to be Rome's first Christian ruler.

During the period of eclipse, the Church in Rome had mightily increased, and so therefore had its meeting-places. Since these meeting-places were, or at any moment might be, proscribed, they were bound to be obscure. Burial-places

94 'The House of the Blessed Virgin' near Ephesus, another claimant for the tomb of Mary. The building was identified in 1891 from the very exact description given by a German nun following a vision fifty years earlier.

were different. Rome had nothing against dead Christians any more than against any other sort of extinct Roman. The idea that the catacombs were 'secret shrines' is wholly false. To start with they were all outside the walls, by the sides of main roads for the most part, and so in full view of any watcher on the ramparts or by the wayside. Secondly, except for a very few small mortuary chapels, there is no space in a catacomb which permits the assembly of more than a small congregation.

The catacombs are of interest to us because they do contain, in eloquent fashion, the earliest known examples of Christian art. The subjects rendered in simple frescoes are the Eucharist, praying figures, the Good Shepherd, Old Testament prototypes of Christ, or Christ himself, sometimes in the guise of Orpheus or the Sun. The oldest catacomb in Rome is that of Priscilla, on the Salarian Way. At least fifteen others, in addition to three Jewish ones, have been identified.

95 *below*. Carthage. The remains of the Basilica of Saint Cyprian who was martyred here in the year 253.

96 *below right*. The catacombs in Rome were burial places not secret meeting places. They were decorated with frescoes representing such subjects as the Eucharist, praying figures, Old Testament prototypes of Christ, and the Lord himself sometimes in the guise of deities such as Orpheus or the Sun or, as here, the Good Shepherd. This picture is in the catacomb of Priscilla on the Salarian Way, the oldest catacomb in Rome, dating from the second and third centuries.

The meeting-places where the faithful assembled for worship were all originally house-churches.

A magnificent series of funeral grottoes was brought to light beneath St Peter's itself during the decade 1940–50. The earliest are pagan memorials in a cemetery of some grandeur. Much of the area was cut away and levelled when Constantine dedicated the site to the great basilica he was to build over the tomb of St Peter himself. From the remainder of the grottoes it is clear that the tomb of St Peter was venerated in this very spot as early as the second century. Many graffiti incised by early pilgrims testify to the sanctity of the place.

If now we turn our eyes to the east, we note that the Church of Egypt, today represented by the Coptic communion, traces its origin to the labours of St Mark. It very early rose to commanding eminence, specially through its anchorites, who will be considered in the next section. The Orthodox Church of Ethiopia may be dated, not to the

97 One of the earliest Christian mosaics in the Grotto of the 'Tomb of Saint Peter' beneath the Vatican. It shows Christ wearing the radiate crown and in the chariot of the sun-god. A fascinating example of the gradual approach of solar monotheism to Christian monotheism.

Ethiopian Treasurer baptized by Philip (page 78), but to the year 341, when a certain Frumentius on a journey from Tyre with his brother was captured at an Ethiopian port, and sent to King Ezana at Aksum, which is still the spiritual centre of Ethiopia. For long the Ethiopian Church was dependent on the Coptic Church of Egypt, but since 1959, it has been completely autocephalous, with its own patriarchate.

Rome, not only as the capital of the known world, but because its Church could claim to have been founded not by one apostle, but by two, Peter and Paul, was bound to claim primacy. When Constantine founded his new capital on the Bosphorus, on the site of ancient Byzantium, he called it 'New Rome' but it was also known as Constantinopolis. It was built, said its founder, 'by command of God', to whom it was solemnly dedicated on 11 May 330. From the first it was a Christian city, unsullied by any pagan cult or rite.

98 A restored fourth-century mosaic from the Church of Santa Pudenziana in Rome, showing Christ in glory surrounded by the Apostles and the symbols of the Evangelists. Quite clear on either side are the buildings of Constantinian Jerusalem: Calvary as it then was, open to the sky; on the right the triple portal of the Church of the Martyrion and on the left the Rotunda which covered the tomb.

99 *opposite*. Hippo Regius in what is now Algeria where Saint Augustine taught and died. In the foreground the remains of the ancient city, in the background the modern church of Saint Augustine.

100 *below*. The ruined façade of Saint Paul's Church in Macao, China. The Church was built by Japanese Christians in 1602 following the mission of Saint Francis Xavier, and was destroyed during a typhoon in 1935.

101 *below right*. Goa, India. Procession through the streets with the body of Saint Francis Xavier, the Jesuit missionary to the East who died in 1552.

Constantine could claim that his realm was now under Christian dominion, even though its population was still predominantly pagan; but he was not the first to found a national Church or a national Christian state. That honour belongs to Armenia. In the year 287 Tiridates III, who had been brought up in Rome, was established as king by Roman arms. He was converted to the Christian faith by St Gregory the Illuminator, and established Christianity as the state religion, preceding Constantine by thirty years. It is still the national faith, and the 'Catholicos of all the Armenians' still resides at Echmiadzin, which has been the national capital since the year 163.

No national Church has ever been established in Persia, or India, or China; and yet in all three countries the exploits of Christian missionaries were remarkable. Nestorius was a man of great force and eloquence who became patriarch of Constantinople in the fifth century, but was later condemned for what were regarded as heretical views about the nature of Christ. His followers evangelized Persia, and even reached China. The four daughters-in-law of Genghis Khan (1167–1227) were all Nestorian Christians; so also was the wife of Hulagu, his grandson. It was only with the collapse of the Mongol empire in the fourteenth century that Chinese Christianity, its protégé and ally, disintegrated too.

In India the Christian message is indissolubly associated with the name and life of St Francis Xavier, the 'Apostle of the Indies'. He was one of Ignatius Loyola's first associates, a Navarrese Basque, and his shrine in Goa is still much frequented. But it was in the island of Shang-ch'uan near the mouth of the Canton river that he died in 1552, at the early age of forty-six, having hoped in vain to be admitted

102 *above*. Saint Francis Xavier's Memorial Church built at Kagashima on Kyushu in 1949, the 400th anniversary of his landing.

103 *opposite*. Madras, India, the shrine of Saint Thomas the Apostle who travelled to the East.

to China. He had previously visited Japan, the first Christian missionary to do so, and despite later vicissitudes, his faith was never extinguished, and Kyushu, where he first worked, is still a Catholic stronghold.

It was on his way to the Far East that St Francis Xavier visited Madras, and it was there that he became convinced of his mission to the East Indies. For Madras was already a Holy Place: it had been known for centuries before the advent of the Portuguese as *Beit Touma*, the House of Thomas, and was not only an important staging-post on the Arab sea-route to Canton, but a shrine venerated as the tomb of the apostle Thomas, the first of the apostles to declare his belief in the divinity of Christ. According to tradition, St Thomas had reached India in the year AD 53, that is seven years before Paul reached Rome, and suffered martyrdom there at the hands of the king of Mylapore. His burial-place is marked by the cathedral of San Thomé, and a chapel dedicated to him stands on St Thomas' Mount. The Church of the East was later active in southern India; and today it is estimated that the Malabar Christians, as they are known, number not less than five million.

9 Monks and Missionaries

OF ALL the influences that have created Holy Places for Christendom, after the lives and works of Jesus and his apostles, none has been more potent than the monastic life; and so to it and its abodes the remaining chapters of this essay will be chiefly devoted.

The Christian monastic movement was the product of the East and of the desert. From the days of Moses to those of Muhammad the desert was the nursery of souls. John the Baptist had preached in the wilderness. Jesus had retired to the desert. So had Paul.

It was in Egypt that the monastic movement had its origin. The first 'monks', that is solitaries (Greek *monos*, alone) were what we should now call hermits, living in caves or tombs, such as may be seen in the wadis of the wilderness between Jerusalem and the Jordan, with evidence of recent habitation. The first Egyptian recluses were similarly housed. It was only in the fourth century that the communal, what we should now call 'monastic', life was organized. The founder of the Christian hermetic discipline was St Antony. Born in Middle Egypt about 250, he began to lead an ascetic life at the age of twenty. After fifteen years, he withdrew to a lonely mountain by the Nile called Pispir, now Deir al Maimun. Hermits began to imitate him, and in the opening years of the fourth century Antony left his retreat to organize their monastic life. Later on he again withdrew, this time to a mountain by the Red Sea. Here the monastery of St Antony and St Paul of Thebes, his companion, commemorates his name. It is the largest of the Coptic desert monasteries, a miniature village, surrounded with a wall of from thirty to fifty feet high. Portions of the buildings go back to the third century.

Antony may justly be styled the 'first monk'. The rule that bears his name (it is still observed by Coptic, Syrian and Armenian monks) was compiled principally from writings and discourses attributed to him in the *Life* by Athanasius. The Latin version of this work, made about 361, and used by St Augustine among others, was the medium by which eastern ascetic ideas reached the western world.

104. The wilderness of Judaea, dwelling place of some of the earliest hermits

The main feature of this type of monachism was its voluntariness. Some men lived as hermits, out of sight or sound of each other, assembling only for services on Saturdays and Sundays. Other monks such as those in the still famous Wadi Natrun, just south of the main Cairo-Alexandria road, lived as a community, and engaged in useful work, as bakers, weavers and gardeners, as physicians even. About the year 1000 there were fifty monasteries in the valley. There are still four, the most important being that known as the Syrian.

The primitive monks, even in the settlements of Wadi Natrun and Skete, retained something of their hermetic life. The word 'skete' is still in use on Mount Athos to mean a detached monastic dwelling. After 1500 years the Holy

105 *right*. Coptic monastery in the Wadi Natrun, Egypt.

106 *opposite*. Lalibella, Ethiopia. The sunken church of Biet Giorgis was carved from solid rock.

108 *above*. Docheiariou Monastery, Mount Athos.

107 *opposite*. The Holy Mountain of Mount Athos. There are still twenty monasteries there, the first having been founded in the tenth century. This picture shows Kapsokalývia, 'village of hermits'.

Mountain still retains a number of Antonian characteristics, notably its leaving to the individual the choice of what degree of solitude to adopt.

Definite organization on standard lines was imposed on the Antonian associations by a certain Pachomius, who founded his first monastery in the second decade of the fourth century near Denderah in Southern Egypt. When he

110 *opposite*. Saint Catherine's Monastery, Sinai. The buildings are surrounded by a fortified wall.

109 *below*. Mar Saba Monastery, founded by Saint Saba of Cappadocia in the fifth century. In its heyday it contained 5000 monks and was a centre for theological literature and poetry.

died in 346, no less than 3000 monks, housed in nine monasteries, acknowledged his rule. There was also a house for women. By the end of the century we are told that there were 7000 Pachomian monks. There were also by this time monastic, or semi-monastic, foundations other than those in Egypt. The great monastery of St Catherine in Sinai, centre of the smallest of the autocephalous churches which make up the Orthodox Eastern Church, acquired great renown from the patronage of the emperor Justinian, who founded it in 527. It stands more than 5000 feet above sea level. It is doubly famous, for its superb mosaics, recently restored to view, and as being the former repository of the Codex Sinaiticus, taken in 1859 by Tischendorf to St Petersburg and now in the British Museum. The monastery harbours the traditional site of the Burning Bush (Exodus 3.2), and those who approach that chapel must take off their shoes before entering.

113 *opposite*. Inside Saint Mary's Church at Goreme.

111 *below*. The Meteora Monasteries in Thessaly, Greece. 'Meteora' means 'mid-air' since formerly access to them was only by a winch and basket (still used for hauling up goods). The monks moved here for safety during the thirteenth century when Thessaly was menaced by the Serbs.

112 *right*. Goreme, Cappadocia, a rock church of the ninth century when an unusually large proportion of the population lived in monastic communities. Cappadocia also produced many of the fourth-century Fathers including Basil of Caesarea, Gregory of Nyssa and Gregory of Nazianzus.

The Cappadocian city of Caesarea, now Kayseri, produced the man who was to be, and still remains, the stabilizer and pattern of Eastern monasticism, namely St Basil (circa 330–379). He has well been called a Roman among the Greeks, because of his care for organization and conservatism in preference to speculation. After visiting monastic houses in Egypt and Syria, he founded his own monastery on the family property in Cappadocia, and for it composed his *Longer* and *Shorter Rules*. We should note specially this word *Rule*. He did not found an 'Order' in the catholic, western sense. To this day, there are no orders in the Eastern Church, and the men and women who adopt the monastic life still observe St Basil's rule, the women habited as they appear in mediaeval mosaics. By the early middle ages, monasticism was firmly rooted in both western and eastern Christendom.

114 *above*. Saint Martin's Cross and the church of Iona Abbey, Scotland, to which Saint Columba came in the first flowering of Irish Christianity.

The monastic idea had been slow in moving west. It came to its full flower in Provence and Aquitaine, where its focus and inspiration were furnished by St Martin of Tours, who in 360 founded the first monastery in Gaul at Ligugé near Poitiers, and later the great house of Marmoutier. Hence his disciples radiated far and wide. They reached Ireland, and from Ireland went to the Western Isles, and to the 'Celtic fringe' of Britain. These missionaries not only carried with them the Faith, they carried also a very high culture.

Celtic monasticism, after crossing from Ireland to Britain, found a home in Iona, under St Columba, and then, moving southward, at Melrose and Lindisfarne with Aidan and Cuthbert. In 849 the relics of St Columba were removed for safety to Kells in Ireland. The abbey church fell into desuetude in the sixteenth century, but by the initiative of the eighth Duke of Argyll restoration started in 1899, and the abbey was reopened for worship in 1912.

115 *opposite*. A page from the Book of Kells, the beautiful eighth-century illuminated Irish gospels.

That the Faith had reached Britain before the days of Columba is beyond question; but after the onslaughts of the Norsemen and Vikings Christianity dwindled and perished throughout the greater part of the land. When Gregory I chose the monk Augustine of St Andrew's in Rome in 596 to convert the British it was to an almost wholly pagan Britain that he sent him. Thus Canterbury as the city where the torch was rekindled has ever since been regarded as holding the primacy of all England and its Church.

Just as Eastern monasticism had needed a Basil to give it coherence and stability, so, two centuries later, did its Western counterpart find a similar co-ordinator in Benedict of Nursia, generally known as St Benedict. St Benedict did

116 *above*. The Benedictine monastery at Melk, Austria, which overlooks the Danube. Its library contains a ninth-century manuscript of a work by Bede.

117 *right*. The Monastery at Subiaco, Italy, the original retreat of Saint Benedict.

not found the Benedictine Order. What he did was to fashion and transmit a Rule, so wise, so comprehensive that it is still the guide not only of the Benedictine Order but of many others, such as the Cistercians. The 'Benedictines' acquired their name only in the late fourteenth century, on the analogy of the Franciscans, founded by St Francis of Assisi in 1210, and the Dominicans founded by the Spanish monk Dominic in 1215; but the Rule of St Benedict had by that time already produced an amazing harvest. Benedict himself had started his creative work at Subiaco, in a lovely valley forty miles east of Rome, which had formerly sheltered one of the emperor Nero's villas, and had continued it at Cassino, half way between Rome and Naples.

118 *above*. Assisi, birth-place and home of Saint Francis.

119 *right*. Saint Francis preaching before Pope Honorius III.

121 *above*. Glastonbury Abbey,
Somerset, England, associated
with the Arthurian legend. The first
church at Glastonbury was supposed
to have been built by Joseph of
Arimathaea, whose staff, when planted
in the ground, sprouted and became
the Glastonbury Thorn flowering at
Christmas. It was also believed
that Joseph of Arimathaea
brought hither the Holy Grail.

120 *opposite*. Tintern Abbey, Monmouthshire, a great Cistercian house
ruined at the dissolution of the
monasteries by Henry VIII. The
countryside around Tintern was an
inspiration for the great Romantic
poet, William Wordsworth, who heard
here 'the still, sad music of humanity'.

It was from the union of Celtic and Roman, that is
Benedictine, cults and cultures that there sprang the
Northumbrian achievement. In Britain itself, Melrose, a
colony of St Aidan's priory of Lindisfarne founded in 635,
maintained the vigour of Celtic Christianity. This met the
Roman, Benedictine, stream at Jarrow and Ripon. The
results of this union were felt far beyond Britain. Willibrord
was the evangelist of what are now the Netherlands and
Belgium; Wynfrith, more familiar as Boniface of Crediton,
became the even more renowned apostle of Germany.
Alcuin, born near York in about 732, not only became
under Charlemagne 'the schoolmaster of Europe', but laid
the foundation of the Latin missal. He died as abbot of
Tours in 804. One begetter of this famous breed, if not the
sole begetter, had been yet another Northumbrian who
represents the fine flower of Anglo-Saxon Christianity but a
century after the arrival of Augustine in Canterbury. His
name was Bede, born in or near Wearmouth in 672. Bede
illuminated the whole of Western Europe.

The darkest of the dark centuries was the ninth; but then
in the tenth (910) was founded the abbey of Cluny, in
Burgundy. It was to be one of the greatest of Benedictine
foundations. By the middle of the eleventh century more
than one thousand Cluniac houses were to be found in
western Europe, save in Britain and south Germany.

During the eleventh century the three great orders, Franciscans, Dominicans and Benedictines, were to be mightily reinforced by two others, founded almost simultaneously, namely the Carthusians, inspired by St Bruno of Cologne in 1086 and the Cistercians who started their mission in the town of Citeaux in Burgundy (from which they take their name) in 1098. The Carthusians took theirs from Chartreuse, a mountain valley north of Grenoble, anglicized as Charterhouse. The Carthusian rule is the strictest in the Roman Catholic Church. There are now about twenty-five such houses in the world. Those of Florence and of Pavia are internationally renowned.

The Cistercians spread far and rapidly, more rapidly in fact than any other order. They were splendidly organized, largely by the Englishman Stephen Harding, and persuasively invigorated by St Bernard of Clairvaux. It was the hey-day of the Crusading spirit; and the orderly enterprise of the Cistercian rule made a direct appeal to those who were tired of the cramping squalor of many a mediaeval town.

122 *above opposite*. The great Abbey at Cluny, centre of the 'Cluniac' reforms which led to the re-ordering and revival of mediaeval monasticism.

123 *below opposite*. La Grande Chartreuse, France, is a successor of the hermitage established in the Chartreuse Valley by Saint Bruno from Cologne in 1084. He went there for seclusion, hard work and prayer.

124 *below*. The island of Tinos, Greece. Worshippers in the church which contains the miraculous Ikon of the Virgin.

In 1662 a former courtier called Armand de Rance decided that the Cistercian Order, great though it was, had become too lax. He therefore founded at La Trappe in France a Cistercian house of the Stricter Observance. There are now some seventy 'Trappist' abbeys spread over the world, where the monks observe a rule of silence, abstain from flesh, fish and eggs, and cultivative orchards and vineyards. This strict order still attracts many adherents today.

By the end of the Middle Ages, the map of Europe, in terms of Holy Places, resembled a Pointilliste picture. From Scotland to Spain from Germany to Italy they stood; even Poland, on the fringe of the East, had its own shrine after 1382, when the veneration of the famous ikon of the Virgin was instituted at Czestochowa. The ikon is to the Eastern Church far more than a sainted image is to the West. The ikon, as its name says, is the express image, the very likeness of the holiness which it mediates. To venerate an ikon is to be in communion with the holy itself.

126 *opposite*. The famous twelfth-century Ikon of Vladimir showing the God-bearer or Madonna, now in a Moscow gallery.

Among the most famous ikons are those of Our Lady at Tinos, in the Aegean, and of Our Lady of Vladimir in Russia – the latter the prototype of many another which has brought solace and hope to the devout in many lands.

With the death of St Bernard in 1153, monasticism's summer had turned to autumn, still fruitful but no longer the warming glory it had been. By the year 1500 the whole monastic idea had been actively attacked. Wyclif had started the assault in 1366. Erasmus and Luther were to follow. In the year 1492 Columbus crossed the Atlantic: within twenty years the Portuguese had journeyed to India and the East. From the rising and the setting sun came calls to adventure which would fire the young and ardent with far more alluring prospects of gain in this life than of treasure in the next.

125 *below*. Apse of the ruined Crusader church at Emwas, close to the modern Trappist monastery of Latrun.

It might well have seemed that the days of monasticism, of veneration of Holy Places, were at an end. In fact they were not. On the contrary the cult of the pilgrimage, and the demand for Holy Places for pilgrims to visit, was about to enter its most flourishing epoch.

10 'Then longen folk to goon on pilgrimages'

127 *opposite*. Canterbury Cathedral, part of a window in the Chapel of Saint Thomas believed to represent Saint Thomas à Becket.

128 *below*. John Lydgate and pilgrims leaving Canterbury, from an early sixteenth-century manuscript of Lydgate's poems.

THIS LINE from Chaucer's *Canterbury Tales* (1388) is one of the most familiar in English poetry.

In 333 the Bordeaux Pilgrim described his visit to the Holy Places; and about seventy years later the Spanish nun, Aetheria, not only gives us an invaluable account of the ceremonies and observances of the sacred sites of both Old and New Testaments in Egypt, Palestine and Syria, but also describes the system of guides and hostels which already served the pilgrims' needs.

130 *opposite*. The Cologne Reliquary, an exquisite gold tabernacle encrusted with jewels, was said to hold the relics of the Magi, the Wise Men. It made Cologne Cathedral a major centre of pilgrimage through the Middle Ages.

129 *below*. The Pilgrim's Way above Godmersham. The road runs from Winchester to Canterbury where Henry II did public penance for his part in Becket's murder in 1174. A shrine erected there in 1175 was a focal point of pilgrimage until it was destroyed in 1538.

Long ere this Europe already had its own Holy Places. The second century shrine of St Peter in Rome, with abundant graffiti of that and the following century, has already been mentioned (page 96). The Roman liturgical calendar for the year 354 names no less than 29 local sanctuaries at which the faithful annually assembled.

Two sinister innovations were to transform the cult of pilgrimages. The first of these was the demand for relics; then in the twelfth century there arose the granting of Indulgences, a form of spiritual discount more easily acquired than comprehended. Relics and Indulgences went together; but so did the demand for more and more Holy Places to serve as the focus of both.

Chaucer's Wyfe of Bath knew all about them. This devout lady had been to Jerusalem three times and of course she had been to Rome. Not content with these pious peregrinations, the Wyfe had also visited Cologne, because that famous city housed the relics of the Magi, and Boulogne and Compostela as well.

132 *above*. The beautiful town of Conques, one of the staging posts on the pilgrim way to Compostela.

Of all the mediaeval pilgrim-shrines, by far the most famous, and the most curious in origin, is that of Santiago de Compostela, not far from Cape Finisterre in north-western Spain. For Dante, writing in 1293 (*Vita Nuova* XL.7) the Holy Land, Santiago and Rome are the three chief attractions. In Bethlehem as already recorded (page 18) St James of Compostela is at home by the mid-twelfth century. Even more remarkable is the exquisite 12th century carving in the Dominican (now Benedictine) abbey at Silos, near Burgos, which shows the Road to Emmaus, with the two disciples and the risen Lord. In this relief, the Lord himself, because he is on a pious journey, is shown in the habit of a pilgrim, with his staff and his scrip bearing the shell which was the distinguishing badge of Santiago. How had this universal popularity and prestige been achieved?

It arose in the following way, and is an instance of demand creating supply.

131 *opposite*. An aerial view of Vézelay, France, showing the structure of the majestic Abbey, one of the starting points for the pilgrimage to the shrine of Santiago de Compostela.

In the year 711 the Muslim general Tariq crossed the narrow strait from Africa and established the first Islamic state in Europe. This state expanded rapidly, with its capital first at Seville and then at Cordoba. The Muslims penetrated into Gothic Gaul, and their advance was only halted in 732 by the victory of Charles Martel at Poitiers.

By the first half of the ninth century Christian Spain was confined to a narrow area in the north of the peninsula. What was needed was a rallying-point, a war-cry for the Christians. Unfortunately Spain, unlike Italy or France, or even Britain, had no martyr's shrine from which the sacred tocsin might sound. When early in the ninth century it became known that some workmen had discovered a 'Roman' tomb near the town of Padron, and had been supernaturally assured that it was none other than the tomb of St James, the story and the relics were eagerly taken up, and the shrine of Santiago came into being. There is absolutely no evidence whatever that St James ever visited Spain: the legend only became current in the seventh century. Still less is it credible that the body of St James, who, as recorded in Acts 12.2, suffered death in Jerusalem, should have been removed to one of the remotest corners of the Roman dominions. No matter: Christian Spain now had its rallying-point, for the long and arduous struggle of the 'Reconquest' which lay ahead. Alfonso II of Asturias (791–842) built a wooden church over the tomb, which Alfonso III (864–910) replaced with a stone one. The town which grew up round the shrine was destroyed in 997 by the caliph Al-Mansur of Cordoba, but the shrine was spared. Eighty years later Alfonso VI of Leon and Castile began the building of the present church. Alfonso had married the daughter of the

133 *right*. The pilgrim road to Santiago crossed the river of Orbigo in the Province of Leon on this picturesque bridge called the Puenta Passa Honrosso.

134 *opposite*. Saint James of Compostela, dressed as a pilgrim, from a fourteenth-century French manuscript (MS Douce 245, f396v).

135 *above*. Thirteenth-century statue of Saint James, behind the altar in the cathedral of Compostela. He is seated, holding a pilgrim staff with a golden gourd, and wearing a hooded cape of silver encrusted with diamonds and precious stones.

136 *above right*. The great shrine of Santiago of Compostela on the north-west coast of Spain where the lost tomb of the Apostle Saint James was said to have been found in the year 813. Built in the eleventh century and constantly enlarged and beautified, Compostela, after Jerusalem and Rome, became the greatest goal of pilgrimage in all of Europe.

Duke of Burgundy. By introducing Cluniac reforms, he greatly increased the flow of pilgrims from Western Europe. Five magnificent churches were built along the pilgrim route, at Tours, Conques, Limoges and Toulouse, the fifth being the great new church at Santiago itself, where in the first years of the sixteenth century a sumptuous hostel was built to receive the pilgrims. It is now an hotel.

From Compostela, the pilgrim bound for Rome might cross Spain to Montserrat, above Barcelona on the north-east coast. The monastery stands at an altitude of 2378 feet. It is a Benedictine Abbey, founded in the eleventh century, on a site where hermitages had existed two hundred years earlier. Its fame as a place of pilgrimage spread throughout Europe and later as far as America. Its dramatic position bred many legends; and inspired Wagner in his creation of *Parsifal*. It is still a much frequented pilgrim shrine.

Some very interesting information about itineraries and speeds is given in Miss R. J. Mitchell's *The Spring Voyage* (Murray, 1964). It was possible to reach Venice from Dover in twenty-five days: the usual time allowed for letters was just under four weeks. In 1458 a company of pilgrims left Venice on 15 May. After visiting Rhodes and Cyprus,

137 *above*. Montserrat near Barcelona, Spain, 'The Castle of the Holy Grail'. Tradition attributes the famous image of 'Our Lady of Montserrat' to Saint Luke. Saint Ignatius Loyola hung up his sword here after his conversion. The monastery plays a significant part in Catalonian culture today and in the religious life of modern Spain.

they performed a true and thorough pilgrimage in the Holy Land. They were back in Venice on 6 September. Clearly therefore to have been to Jerusalem three times was the equivalent in those days of going on three Mediterranean cruises today.

Pilgrimages to other shrines continued with unabated zeal. In Britain, besides those already named, Walsingham in Norfolk became the chief centre of Marian devotion, as in our own days it has once again become, having been notably embellished by Greek Orthodox piety. It is visited by pilgrims of many different communions.

In Italy, besides Rome, there was the Volto Santo at Lucca, the tomb of St Francis (died 1226) at Assisi, and the so-called Holy House at Loreto. The tomb of St Antony at Padua – he died in 1231 – is still a major pilgrim resort. France had St Martin at Tours, Mont-Saint-Michel, La Sainte Chapelle, the Marian shrine at Le Puy, and the alleged relics of the Madeleine at Vézélay.

Mont-Saint-Michel is not only one of the best known, because so dramatically situated, fortified monasteries of the thirteenth century, it has also the distinction of having been the first repository of the cult of St Anne. This devotion

138 *above*. Mont-Saint-Michel,
Normandy, France.

139 *opposite*. Paris, Sainte Chapelle,
the delicate, lavishly decorated chapel
built by Saint Louis IX in 1245 to
house the Crown of Thorns and many
other sacred relics acquired by this
crusading king.

had been imported from Egypt, where, as a recently recovered Greek inscription attests, it had flourished as far
south as Nubia. From Mont-Saint-Michel it reached
Cornwall, and eventually crossed the Atlantic to Sainte-
Anne-de Beaupré in Canada.

The Sainte Chapelle in Paris is the most glorious reliquary
ever devised. It was built between 1243 and 1248 by St
Louis for the devotional needs of the kings of France. He
set out on his Crusade in the following year. The shrine is
in two storeys, the upper of which is sheathed in glass, which
causes the whole building to glow like a gigantic jewel.

The church of La Madeleine at Vézélay is one of the most
perfect of French Romanesque churches. It was here that
St Bernard of Clairvaux preached the Second Crusade, and
here that St Louis took the Cross. It was also a starting-base
for pilgrimages to Compostela.

Germany, in addition to the Magi at Cologne, had the
authentic tomb of Boniface, who was buried at Fulda in
754. In Ireland the tomb of St Patrick at Downpatrick was
a deeply venerated shrine.

The Holy Land itself was still the supreme goal. The
opening of the Danube route, in the early eleventh century,

141 *above*. The popular, modern healing shrine of pilgrimage at Lourdes.

140 *opposite*. Downpatrick, Ireland, traditional site of the grave of Saint Patrick.

greatly facilitated the journey to the Near East. The magnificent Benedictine monastery at Melk, built in 1702, still stands above the waters of the river as a memorial to those bygone wayfarers.

It was the interruption of the pilgrim route by the conquests of the Seljuk Turks in the last quarter of the eleventh century which led to the preaching of the First Crusade. The existence of the Latin Kingdom in the Holy Land made pilgrimages safer once more; and the beautiful little town and part of Acre, north of Mount Carmel, still bear witness to the devotion and splendour of that strange and anomalous era.

The journey was, by modern standards, both hazardous and beset with manifold discomforts. But we may often be surprised at the comparatively speedy manner in which it might be performed. When Margery Kempe set out in 1436 on her pilgrimage to the Great Three shrines, Jerusalem, Rome, and Santiago, she reached Santiago from Bristol in a week. (Chaucer's Wyfe no doubt found that route convenient, too: Bath is only nine miles from Bristol.) Pilgrimages were not universally regarded with favour,

142. Saint Basil's Cathedral, the finest of Moscow's four cathedrals, built by Ivan the Terrible in 1560.

145 *right*. The walled city of Avila, Spain, where Saint Teresa the Carmelite reformer and mystical writer lived nearly all her life (1515–82). The whole city is still pervaded by her wonderful and courageous spirit.

144 *below right*. The tomb of Saint Thérèse of Lisieux, France.

143 *below*. Among the treasures of the splendid library of the Monastery of San Lorenzo (Escorial) near Madrid is this little manuscript book written by Saint Teresa and the saint's own inkwell.

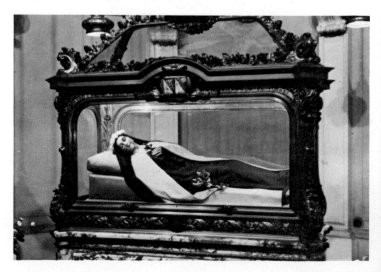

146 *above*. Fatima, Portugal, where three children had six visions of 'Our Lady of the Rosary' in 1917, now a place of pilgrimage for many thousands each year. This stained-glass window depicts the miracle of the sun—one of their visions.

particularly when directed to 'relics'. Augustine himself had condemned the 'hawking about of limbs of martyrs – if indeed they really are martyrs'. The author of *The Imitation of Christ*, in the early fifteenth century, warns that 'they who go much on pilgrimage be seldom made thereby perfect and holy'.

The Reformers of the sixteenth century were totally opposed to pilgrimages, Holy Places, relics, and shrines. The Augsburg Confession of 1530 denounces pilgrimages as 'childish and useless works'. Luther condemned the veneration of relics in 1537. In 1553, the Anglican Articles of Religion stigmatize it as 'a fond thing vainly invented'. In 1538, the shrines of St Thomas at Canterbury and St Cuthbert at Durham had been destroyed.

Despite this setback, the cult of pilgrimages, and the creation of new Holy Places, continued. Mediaeval shrines still attracted devotees, as they do to this day. But new centres had come into being. Some of these were in the Old World, such as that of the Holy Shroud at Turin (1578), St Jean Vianney of Ars (died 1859), Lourdes (1858), St Thérèse (died 1897) of Lisieux, and Fatima in Portugal (1917). Towering above all these saints and sanctuaries, some of whom are to say the least rather dim-haloed, stands the majestic figure of St Teresa of Avila, who died in 1582. To this day, the whole of that bleak upland city seems to be possessed by her mystical, practical power. Avila ranks without question among the true Holy Places of Christendom.

But the New World was now to be inlaid with patines of bright martyr gold. Once again it was the Jesuits who were

147 *right*. Lima, Peru. A relic of the lemon tree planted by Saint Rose, the first canonised saint of America.

148 *below*. Acre, the crypt of Saint John, actually the Crusader refectory beneath the Turkish citadel. Acre, captured in 1104 by Baldwin I, the first King of Jerusalem, was a major Crusader strongpoint and for a hundred years until its fall in 1291, capital of the Crusader kingdom. Through this stronghold, therefore, came the great warrior–pilgrims of the Middle Ages.

the pioneers. Their first 'witness' fell in Florida in 1576. In 1646, eight French Jesuits were martyred by the Iroquois in Canada and New York. They were canonized in 1930.

St Anne de Beaupré in Canada and the great Marian centre of Guadeloupe in Mexico are two of the best known centres of devotion. The first European to reach what is now Arizona was the Franciscan Marcos de Nija, in 1539. The church of St Xavier del Bac in Tucson is the best example of the Spanish Renaissance style north of Mexico. At San Antonio, Texas, stands the cathedral of San Fernando built in 1734. Four Franciscan missions were founded near by. The Franciscan Missions of California (1771–1798) are world-famous.

The disciples of Mary Baker Eddy, who died in 1910, would certainly claim the Mother Church of Christ Scientist in Boston, Massachusetts, as a Holy Place, even if not in the traditional sense; and the members of the Church of Jesus Christ of Latter-Day Saints might make a similar bid for the Temple in Salt Lake City, Utah.

In 1671 the New World was to receive its first saint, when Pope Clement X issued the bill which canonized Isabel de Flores as St Rose of Lima, in Peru.

149. The gigantic figure of Christ the Redeemer at Corcovolo which dominates the landscape at Rio de Janeiro.

11 'The One Remains'

The One remains, the many change and pass,
  Heaven's light for ever shines, earth's shadows die;
Life like a dome of many-coloured glass
  Stains the white radiance of eternity.

IN GENEVA, against a 300-foot wall on the Promenade des Bastions, there stands the Reformation Monument, completed in 1917. It is of great dignity and eloquence. The central group of sculpture consists of statues of Calvin, Farel, Beza and Knox, flanked by figures of others who strove greatly for reformation. Its graven motto is simply *Post Tenebras Lux*, 'after darkness light'.

John Calvin died in Geneva in 1564; and in the four centuries since his death, both the Reformed and Traditional branches of the Church have raised many commanding shrines to the glory of God, both in the Old World and the New. Of definitely Protestant creations, a very large number are in America, whither so many of its first inhabitants had fled from the rigidity and hostility of established religion. The Pilgrim Fathers, first so called by David Webster in 1820, sailed for New England in 1620.

151 *right*. The 'Plimoth Plantation', a replica of the first village established by the Pilgrim Fathers at their landfall.

150 *opposite*. Plymouth, Massachusetts. The rock on which the Pilgrim Fathers first set foot on America in their flight from religious persecution by James I, in 1620.

152. Cambridge, Massachusetts. Christ Church, built in 1761 is one of the finest colonial churches. Washington quartered his troops here in 1775.

There thus arose, in New England especially, a host of small churches, chiefly for Congregational and Unitarian communities, which for grace and aptitude are unsurpassed anywhere in the world. Christ Church, Boston (1723), St Paul's Chapel, New York (1746) and St Michael's, Charleston (1761) are all expressions of the Wren-Gibbs tradition.

This delightful interlude is certainly among Protestantism's most pleasing contribution to the Holy Places of Christendom. Meanwhile, the two main streams of traditional architecture continued to run side by side. Bernini (1598–1680) and Borromini (1599–1667) dominated Roman architecture for the greater part of a century, and firmly established the Baroque (the origin of the word is unknown) as the leading ecclesiastical style. Baroque proliferated all over Europe. Even Russia would know Baroque influence, as in Rastrelli's Smolny Cathedral (1755) in St Petersburg. In Moscow, all four cathedrals – Archangel Michael (1509),

153. San Antonio, Texas, the early eighteenth-century Franciscan mission.

The Assumption (1479), Annunciation (1484) and – most famous of all – St Basil (1560) – were built in the pre-Baroque era, though the first three show the influence of Italian ideas and hands.

With the nineteenth century we enter the epoch of what has been termed the 'Gothic Revival'. The 'revival' started appropriately enough in France, which had given birth to the Gothic style.

In both Britain and the United States Gothic architecture flourished during the nineteenth century. All over England the fine new churches arose. Soon, with Ruskin playing the part which Montalembert had played in France, Gothic was equated with Christian and the kingdom was starred with shrines. Pugin, Butterfield, and later Scott, Street and Waterhouse were the leading church architects of their day.

154 *opposite*. Tucson, Arizona. The Saint Xavier del Bac Mission is the best example of Spanish renaissance church building north of Mexico.

In 1880 J. L. Pearson designed Truro cathedral, the first cathedral to be built in England since Wren's St Paul's. Burges's cathedral in Cork (1876) is still proclaiming the exuberant French style of the twelfth century; but by the end of the nineteenth, church architecture had become much firmer, largely under the influence of such men as Bodley and Shaw. In 1903, Giles Gilbert Scott, grandson of the great Sir George Gilbert Scott, at the age of twenty-three won the competition for the building of a new cathedral in Liverpool. This magnificent church, still unfinished, is splendidly 'firm'. In its initial stages, for example the Lady Chapel, it clearly shows Bodley's influence. Its later development reflects the staunchness of Spanish Romanesque. It is the grand finale to the Gothic pageant in England. Hard by stands the new Roman Catholic cathedral, designed by Frederick Gibberd, on foundations which were intended to support Sir Edwin Lutyens's vast basilica.

155 *right*. Saint Anne de Beaupré, Quebec. The miraculous statue of Saint Anne in a much-visited Canadian shrine.

156 *over*. Midland, Ontario. The shrine of the six Jesuits martyred in 1649 by the Iroquois Indians rises behind a reconstruction of the Huron Indian village and mission station.

157 *above*. Notre Dame de Haut
at Ronchamp built by Le Corbusier
in 1955 follows the twentieth-century
French tradition of allowing great
artists to create cultural and religious
shrines for the modern pilgrim.
Matisse and Chagal have their
memorials too.

English churches sprang up in every continent. Often
these were the centres of missionary endeavour. Among the
most significant is the Anglican cathedral in Zanzibar,
because it stands on the site of the former slave-market
from which David Livingstone set out to convert 'darkest
Africa'.

158 *above*. Nearly 70 years in building, Washington Cathedral nears completion. Many services of national significance in the United States are held here every year.

159 *right*. Riverside Church, New York City, patterned after Chartres Cathedral, has been a centre of Christian social concern ever since its dedication in 1931 under the great American preacher, Harry Emerson Fosdick.

160 *right*. Boston, Massachusetts. Trinity Church built by H. H. Richardson in 1872 marks the birth of an authentic American style of ecclesiastical architecture.

161 *below*. Grace Cathedral, San Francisco, 1910–1966, is built of concrete to withstand seismic shocks.

In America the Gothic revival was inevitably an import; but it was to achieve in the hands of American architects an individuality which would have an influence *à rebours* on English practice. The building of Trinity Church, New York, between 1839 and 1846 established the reputation of its architect, Richard Upjohn. Upjohn had many followers, and a specifically American style began to emerge. The climate of northern America is not unlike that of northern Spain; and so it is natural that American architects should turn to northern Spanish models, that is to Romanesque architecture. This is just what the greatest of American church designers did. His name was Henry Hobson Richardson. The crown of his genius and achievement is his famous Trinity Church on Copley Square in Boston. The interior of this great church is enriched by a number of large memorial windows by John Lafarge, William Morris, Edward Burne-Jones and others. The exterior of its north wall serves as a background to a statue of Phillips Brooks who was for twenty-two years from 1869 the occupant of that church's pulpit. He is the author of the cherished hymn 'O little town of Bethlehem'. Trinity Church is assuredly one of the Holy Places of Christendom.

162. Zanzibar, the Anglican
Cathedral. The high altar is on the site
of the whipping post in Africa's most
notorious slave market. H. M.
Stanley set out from here in 1871 to
find the great Scottish missionary,
David Livingstone.

In 1923 a wholly new concept was introduced into
church-building. The innovation was primarily structural,
but it answered a growing demand for a church that should
channel contemporary devotions in a contemporary way.
In that year the brothers Auguste and Gustave Perret
constructed the church of Notre Dame at Le Raincy on the
outskirts of Paris. It is made entirely of concrete and glass.

The Perrets' revolution permeated the whole of Europe.
Even Corbusier's celebrated church of Notre Dame du
Haut at Ronchamp, France, pays tribute to the Perrets
(1955), being nevertheless of the first importance on its own
merits. They are the most eloquent heralds of a new
Christian age. The nineteenth century, for all its com-

163. Nukapu, Melanesia. This simple cross marks the spot where on 20 September 1871 Bishop Patteson was murdered in mistaken revenge for the kidnapping of some of the islanders by white slave-traders.

placency, had seen the Church ever-militant against evil, not only, as mentioned above, in Europe, but in distant lands as well. John Coleridge Patteson, bishop of Melanesia, who died at Nukapu in the Santa Cruz group in 1871, fell a martyr to this very conflict. The barbarous rapacity of white enslavers had led the simple Islanders to believe that each and every white man, even the man they had known as their gentle pastor before the 'blackbirders' started to raid them, must be in league against their lives. Patteson did not die in vain, because his death hastened the suppression of this vile traffic. It is this practical care for men and women of all races which inspires contemporary Christianity, and informs the places that they endeavour to make holy.

All over Europe and in America too the new cult of light and directness has steadily gained ground. In England its culminating glory is beyond question the cathedral built at Coventry by Sir Basil Spence. This wonderful building, which since its dedication in 1962 has attracted millions of pilgrims, was designed as an act of reconciliation. The old cathedral had been gutted by German bombs; but Christians knew that in Germany itself the flame of self-sacrifice burned bright as well. Among the great latter-day martyrs was numbered Dietrich Bonhoeffer, a Lutheran pastor who taught a theology of a 'church for the world'.

Bonhoeffer was born in 1906 in Breslau, near Wroclaw in Poland. He studied in Berlin under Harnack, and was influenced by Karl Barth. He studied at the Union Theological Seminary in New York, and in 1930–31 lectured on systematic theology at Berlin University. In 1933, after protesting against anti-Jewish laws forced upon the state, the university and later the Church, Bonhoeffer went to London to minister to Lutheran congregations there and to awaken the ecumenical movement to the dangers of Nazism. He returned to Germany in 1935, where he became head of a college founded by the anti-Nazi German Confessing Church. In 1939 he went to New York again, but after only a few weeks he went back to Nazi Germany. He was arrested in 1943 and after two years imprisonment he was hanged at Flossenburg concentration camp in Bavaria on 9 April 1945.

Reconciliation, the theme of Coventry cathedral, was the flower that sprang from Bonhoeffer's grave.

164 *right*. The scene of the martyrdom of German Pastor Dietrich Bonhoeffer at the Flossenberg concentration camp in Bavaria.

165 *opposite*. Coventry, England. The ruins of the mediaeval Cathedral destroyed in the blitz in 1942 are linked with Sir Basil Spence's new Cathedral consecrated in 1962. Epstein's St. Michael is on the right. The theme of the building is Reconciliation.

List of illustrations

1. 'Jacob's Ladder', illumination from the twelfth century Lambeth Bible
2. Bethel, view to Ai
3. Nazareth, general view including the Basilica of the Incarnation
4. Nazareth, Greek Orthodox Church of the Annunciation, the crypt and Mary's Well
5. Nazareth, Greek Catholic Synagogue-Church
6. 'Ain Karim, general view including Church of Saint John
7. 'Ain Karim, Church of the Visitation, grotto and cistern
8. 'Ain Karim, Church of the Visitation, altar
9. Bethlehem, Christmas procession
10. Church of the Nativity, interior
11. Church of the Nativity, detail of column with fresco
12. Church of the Nativity, entrance
13. Church of the Nativity, Crusader stairway to the Grotto of the Nativity
14. Church of the Nativity, Grotto of the Nativity
15. Church of the Nativity, silver star marking the birthplace of Christ
16. Shepherds in the fields near Bethlehem
17. 'Adoration of the Magi', by Hieronymus Bosch (Prado, Madrid)
18. Jerusalem, distant view showing the Temple area
19. Jerusalem, Dome of the Rock, the Sacred Rock
20. Jerusalem, the Western or Wailing Wall
21. 'Flight into Egypt', fresco from the Bellieu Church in Bulgaria
22. Old Cairo, the well of Saint Sergius' Church
23. Pope Paul VI prays over the waters of the River Jordan
24. Mount of Temptation
25. View from Mount of Temptation over Jordan valley
26. Sea of Galilee
27. Capernaum, ruins of the second century synagogue
28. Cana, Galilee
29. 'The Woman of Samaria', fresco from Zillis Church, Switzerland
30. Jacob's Well, Sychar, Samaria
31. Capernaum, Church of the Beatitudes
32. Tabgha, Church of the Primacy, 'Christ's Table'
33. Tabgha, steps down to the lake from the Church of the Primacy
34. Tabgha, traditional site of the Feeding of the Five Thousand
35. Tabgha, Church of the Multiplication of Bread, fifth century mosaic of loaves and fishes
36. Galilee, from the Mount of Beatitudes
37. Mount Tabor
38. Mount Tabor, Basilica of the Transfiguration
39. Map of Jerusalem
40. Bethany, general view
41. Bethany, tomb of Lazarus
42. Palm Sunday procession to Jerusalem from Bethphage
43. Jerusalem, Lion or St Stephen's Gate
44. Jerusalem, view from window of Dominus Flevit shrine
45. Jerusalem, Gethsemane, Church of All Nations and Russian Church of Saint Mary Magdalene
46. Jerusalem, Garden of Gethsemane
47. Jerusalem, Pool of Bethesda and Church of Saint Anne
48. Jerusalem, The Cenacle, Mount Zion
49. Jerusalem, 'Game of the King' paving stone
50. Jerusalem, Convent of the Dames de Zion, ancient Roman pavement
51. Jerusalem, Church of Saint Mark
52. Jerusalem, Saint Peter in Gallicantu, paved street and church
53. Jerusalem, rock-cut cells below the church
54. Church of the Holy Sepulchre, Good Friday procession
55. Jerusalem, Via Dolorosa
56. The Church of the Holy Sepulchre
57. Church of the Holy Sepulchre, east façade and Chapel of Saint Helena from the Lutheran hostel
58. Church of the Holy Sepulchre, domes, and the tower of the Lutheran Church
59. The Madaba Mosaic, showing Jerusalem in the sixth century
60. 'Church of the Holy Sepulchre, Jerusalem' from a fifteenth-century manuscript
61. Church of the Holy Sepulchre, Calvary, the three altars
62. Church of the Holy Sepulchre, Stone of the Anointing
63. Church of the Holy Sepulchre, inside the Tomb
64. Church of the Holy Sepulchre, the entrance to the Tomb
65. Church of the Holy Sepulchre, mediaeval pilgrims' crosses cut into the walls
66. Church of the Holy Sepulchre, the Coptic Chapel at the rear of the Tomb

67. Roman paved way at El-Qubeibeh
68. Jerusalem, the Mount of Olives
69. Jerusalem, the Golden Gate
70. Jerusalem, the Church of the Ascension on the Mount of Olives
71. Jerusalem, the Armenian Cathedral of Saint James
72. 'The Stoning of Stephen', by Beato Angelico (Vatican Museum, Rome)
73. Jerusalem, the Damascus Gate
74. Jaffa, the old town
75. Hebron, Saint Philip's Well
76. Jaffa, a street near the site of Simon the Tanner's house
77. Saint Paul, from a sixth century mosaic in the Arian Baptistry, Ravenna
78. The Cilician Gates
79. Antioch, Saint Peter's Church
80. Antioch, the altar in Saint Peter's Church
81. Cyprus, Saint Barnabas Monastery
82. Cyprus, tomb of Saint Barnabas
83. Pisidia, Lake Egridir
84. Via Egnatia between Kavalla and Philippi
85. Miletus, the theatre
86. Ephesus, the theatre and the Arcadian Way
87. Tyre, shrine and view over harbour
88. Rome, the Tiber with Castel Sant' Angelo and dome of Saint Peter's
89. Caesarea, the ruins of the Roman harbour
90. Malta, Saint Paul's Bay
91. Rome, Church of Saint Paul-without-the-Walls
92. Rome, the sculptured head of Saint Paul in the shrine of the Three Fountains
93. Jerusalem, Tomb of the Virgin
94. Ephesus, Panagia Kapulu, 'House of the Virgin'
95. Carthage, Basilica of Saint Cyprian
96. Rome, Catacomb of Priscilla, fresco of the Good Shepherd
97. Rome, Saint Peter's, the Christ-Helios mosaic
98. Rome, Church of Santa Pudenziana, mosaic
99. Hippo, Algeria, Saint Augustine's Church
100. Macao, China, the façade of Saint Paul's Church
101. Goa, India, procession with the body of Saint Francis Xavier
102. Saint Francis Xavier memorial, Kagashima, Kyushu, Japan
103. Madras, India, Saint Thomas' Mount
104. Wilderness of Judaea
105. Wadi Natrun Monastery, Egypt
106. Lalibella, Ethiopia, the sunken church of Biet Giorgis
107. Kapsokalyvia, a village of hermits and Mount Athos from the sea
108. Docheiariou Monastery, Mount Athos
109. Mar Saba Monastery in the Kedron Valley near Jerusalem
110. Saint Catherine's Monastery, Sinai
111. The Meteora Monasteries in Greece
112. Goreme, Cappadocia, landscape with rock-churches
113. Goreme, Cappadocia, inside St Mary's Church
114. Iona, the Abbey Church and St Martin's Cross
115. Portrait of Christ, from the Book of Kells
116. Melk, Austria, the Benedictine monastery
117. Subiaco, Italy, the Sacro Speco Monastery
118. Assisi, Italy, general view
119. Saint Francis of Assisi, fresco from the crypt of St Francis, at Assisi
120. Tintern Abbey, Monmouthshire
121. Glastonbury Abbey, Somerset
122. Abbaye de Cluny, France
123. Monastery of La Grande Chartreuse, France
124. Tinos, Greece, worshippers at the Miraculous Ikon of the Virgin
125. Emwas, church remains
126. The famous Russian ikon, the Virgin of Vladimir
127. Canterbury Cathedral, the Saint Thomas window
128. Pilgrims on the way to Canterbury, from a sixteenth century manuscript
129. The Pilgrims' Way above Godmersham, Kent
130. Cologne Cathedral, the reliquary
131. Vézélay, France, the Abbey Church of La Madeleine
132. Conques, France, on the pilgrim route to Santiago
133. The Puenta Passa Honrosso in northern Spain
134. Saint James of Compostela dressed as a pilgrim
135. Santiago de Compostela, the shrine of Saint James
136. Santiago de Compostela, the Cathedral
137. The Monastery of Montserrat near Barcelona
138. Mont-Saint-Michel
139. Paris, Sainte Chapelle, the stained glass windows of the upper chapel
140. Downpatrick, Ireland, Saint Patrick's grave
141. Lourdes, a candle-lit gathering of pilgrims at the Basilica
142. Moscow, Saint Basil's Cathedral
143. Saint Teresa's book and inkwell, now in the Escorial Library
144. Lisieux, the shrine of Sainte Thérèse
145. Avila, the ancient city walls
146. Fatima, the Miracle of the Sun window
147. Lima, Peru, relic of a lemon tree at the shrine of Saint Rose
148. Acre, the Crypt of Saint John
149. Rio de Janeiro, statue of Christ the Redeemer
150. Plymouth, Massachusetts, the Plymouth Rock
151. Plymouth, Massachusetts, Plimoth Plantation, a replica of the first Pilgrim Fathers' village
152. Cambridge, Massachusetts, Christ Church
153. San Antonio, Texas, the Espada Mission
154. Tucson, Arizona, the Saint Xavier del Bac Mission
155. Saint Anne de Beaupré, Quebec, the Miracle Statue
156. Saint Marie among the Hurons, Midland, Ontario, the Jesuit Martyrs' shrine
157. Ronchamp, France, the chapel by Le Corbusier
158. Washington Cathedral
159. Riverside Church, New York
160. Boston, Massachusetts, the Trinity Church
161. San Francisco, Grace Cathedral
162. Zanzibar, the altar in the Anglican Cathedral
163. Nukapu, Melanesia, memorial cross to Bishop Patteson
164. Flossenburg Camp, Germany
165. Coventry Cathedral

Acknowledgements

Very many people have given me generous help in the preparation of this book. In particular I want to thank the following: The Hon. Mabel Strickland; Alistair Duncan of the Middle East Archive; John Stockdale my editor at Mowbrays; Mrs Jenny Turtle, who assembled the pictures; The Revd Gerard Bushell, OFM, author of *Churches of the Holy Land* and, as so many times before, The Revd Joseph Crehan, SJ.

Acknowledgements and thanks are due to the following for the use of illustrations:
Revd J. C. Allen 4, 22, 24, 52, 92, 146; Australian Board of Missions 163; Helmut Bock 164; The Bodleian Library, Oxford 134; Anne Bolt 90, 145; British Library Board 60; British Tourist Authority 120, 121, 127, 140; Camera Press 9 (photo: Werner Braun), 88 (photo: Wim Swaan); J. Allen Cash 137, 142; Richard Cleave 18, 19, 39; Colorific 23 (photo: Terence le Goubin), 124 (photo: Philip Boucas); Prof. Kenneth J. Conant 56; D. Dickens 100, 111, 151, 156; Robert Estall 116, 133, 136, 155; French Government Tourist Office 122, 131, 138; Sonia Halliday 21, 29, 78, 79, 80, 81, 82, 83, 84, 85, 113; Tom Hanley 103; Robert Harding Associates 47, 86, 105, 110; Michael Holford 17, 95, 128, 143; Angelo Hornak 152, 160; Italian State Tourist Office 91; Japan National Tourist Organisation 102; Seán Jennett 129; Jerusalem and the Middle East Church Association 30; Victor Kennett 153, 154; A. F. Kersting 114, 139, 165; Lambeth Palace Library 1; Lauros-Giraudon 123; Magnum 101 (photo: Bruno Barbey); Janet March-Penney 135, 150; Middle East Archive front cover, 2, 6, 7, 8, 10, 11, 12, 13, 14, 16, 25, 26, 34, 44, 45, 49, 51, 53, 54, 55, 56, 57, 58, 59, 61, 62, 65, 66, 67, 68, 71, 73, 74, 75, 87, 104, 109, 125; William McQuitty 149; Novosti 126; Office Central de Lisieux 144; Picturepoint 38, 42, 46, 106, 157, 161; George Rainbird Ltd. 97 (photo: Mario Carrieri); Ianthe Ruthven 5, 15, 28, 31, 33, 37, 40, 41, 43, 48, 50, 64, 70, 76, 93; Scala, Florence 72, 77, 96, 98, 117, 130; Toni Schneiders 118, 119; Ronald Sheridan title page, 3, 20, 27, 35, 36, 63, 69, 89, 148; Reresby Sitwell 107, 108, back cover; I. Sobadjeff 94, 112; Spectrum 141; Revd A. Talbot-Ponsonby 32; Trinity College Dublin 115; United Society for the Propagation of the Gospel 162; Christopher Neal Wallis 147; Roger Wood 99

Index

Abyssinians 66, 104
Acre 15, 87, 140
Adonis 16
Aetheria 39, 52, 54
Aidan, Saint 112, 117
'Ain Karim 12, 13
Aksum 97
Alcuin 117

Anne, Saint, church of 51, 52
Antioch, Syria 83, 84
Antioch, Pisidia 84
Antonia, Tower of 52, 89
Antony, Saint, of Egypt 103
Antony, Saint, of Padua 132
Armenian Church 16, 25, 74, 99
Arnon 15

Assisi 132
Assyrians 25
Athos, Mount 104, 107
Augustine, Saint, of Hippo 81, 103, 135
Augustine, Saint, of Canterbury 114, 117

Baldwin, kings 18, 51, 140
Barluzzi, A. 15, 23, 52
Barnabas, Saint 83
Basil, Saint 110, 114, 145
Beaupré, Saint Anne de 132, 141
Becket, Saint Thomas à 123, 124, 139
Bede, Venerable 117
Benedict, Saint 114, 115
Bernadette, Saint 135
Bernard of Clairvaux, Saint 118, 120, 135
Bethany 45 seq.
Bethel 7, 8
Bethlehem 15 seq.
Bethphage 45, 46
Bonhoeffer, D. 154
Booth, General W. 81
Bordeaux Pilgrim 35, 62
Boston, Massachusetts
    Mother Church of Christ Scientist 141
    Trinity Church 151
Boulogne 124
Bruno, Saint 118, 119

Caesarea 78, 89, 91, 110
Calvin 143
Cambridge, Massachusetts
    Christ Church 144
Cana 34
Capernaum 33, 34, 37, 43
Carmel, Mount 42
Carthage 94, 95
Carthusians 118
Catacombs 95
Catherine, Saint, monastery of (Sinai) 108
Charlemagne, emperor 16, 117
Charleston, Saint Michael's Church 144
Chaucer 123, 124
Cistercians 115, 118
Cluny 117, 119
Cologne 124
Columba, Saint 112
Columbus 120
Compostela 18, 124, 127 seq., 135
Constantine, emperor 16, 61, 62, 93, 94, 96, 97, 99
Coptic Church 66, 96, 97, 104
Corbusier 149, 152
Cornelius 79
Couasnon, Rev. Charles, OP 65
Coventry 154
Cuthbert, Saint 112, 139
Cyprian, Saint 94, 95
Cyprus 83
Czestochowa 119

Dames de Zion 52
Diocletian, emperor 94
Dominicans 115
Dominus Flevit 47, 48
Downpatrick 135

Eddy, Mrs Mary Baker 141
Emmaus 73, 127
Erasmus 120
Eudokia, empress 77
Eusebius 62

Fatima 139
Felicity, Saint 94
Franciscans 11, 12, 13, 23, 47, 48, 54, 79, 115

Galilee 33 seq.
Gallicantu, church of Saint Peter in 54
Gethsemane 47, 48
Gibberd, 7, 147
Gothic Revival 145, 146
Gregory, Saint, the Illuminator 99
Gregory I, Pope 114

Hadrian, emperor 16, 61, 62, 88
Helena, Saint 16, 61, 65, 66, 70, 73
Herod the Great 15, 27, 29, 30, 89
Hermon, Mount 30, 42
Holy Sepulchre, Church of 54, 59 seq.
Holy Shroud (Turin) 139
House-churches in Rome 96

Ignatius Loyola, Saint 81, 99, 131

Jacob's Well 34, 35
Jaffa (Joppa) 79
Jericho 31, 45
Jerome, Saint 16, 20, 23
John the Baptist, Saint 30, 103
Jordan, river 30, 31, 45
Justin Martyr 16
Justinian, emperor 16, 23, 108

Kedron valley 62
Kells 112
Komnenos of Mitylene 66

Le Raincy 152
Lindisfarne 117
Liverpool, cathedrals in 147
Loreto 132
Louis, Saint 79, 132, 135
Lourdes 135, 139
Lucca 132
Luther 120, 139

Madaba Map 61, 62, 74
Madras 100
Magi, The 124
Malta 91
Mark, Saint, Church of 51, 52
Martin of Tours, Saint 112, 132
Megiddo 42
Melisende, Queen 51
Melk 135
Mont-Saint-Michel 132
Montserrat 130, 131
Moscow 136, 144-5

Nazareth 11, 12
Nebo, Mount 15
Nero, emperor 91, 93
Nestorius 99
New York
    Saint Paul's Chapel 144
    Trinity Church 151

Olives, Mount of 37, 73
Origen 94

Pachomius 107, 108
Paul, Saint 81, 91 seq.
Paul VI, Pope 30, 65
Pentecost 73, 74
Perga 84
Perpetua, Saint 94
Perret, Auguste and Gustave 152
Persians 16, 62
Peter, Saint 78, 79
Philip, Saint 78, 79
Philippi 84
Pilgrim Fathers 143
Pilgrimages denounced 139
Pliny 29
Pudenziana, Saint, Church of 62

Reformation Monument, Geneva 143
Relics 124, 135, 139
Richardson, H. H. 151
Rome 89, 91, 93 seq., 124
Rose of Lima, Saint 140, 141
Russian Christians 79

Salt Lake City 141
Santiago de Compostela 127 seq.
Saul of Tarsus (see also Paul) 77, 78
Scott, Sir G. G. 147
Scott, Giles G. 147
Simon the Tanner 79
Spence, Sir Basil 154
Stephen, Saint 77
Syrian Christians 25, 52, 66

Tabor, Mount 39, 42
Temple, the, of Jerusalem 26-29
Temptation, Mount of 30, 31
Teresa of Avila, Saint 138, 139
Thérèse of Lisieux, Saint 138, 139
Thomas, Saint 100
Trappists 119
Tyre and Sidon 37, 87

Vatican Grottoes 96
Vézélay 127, 132, 135
Via Dolorosa 52, 54, 56
Virgin's Tomb, the 93

Wadi Natrun 104
Walsingham 130
Wesley, John 81
Willibrord, Saint 117
Wren, Sir Christopher 144, 147
Wyclif 120
Wynfrith (Boniface of Crediton) 117, 135

Xavier, Saint Francis 99, 100

Zanzibar 149, 152

2 MAR 1979

Vers cestes parties ço est a sauoz

...ame de sardaine

...damasceno
...et dno suo
...cordie qngetas
libraz argenti

seignur A crucifier
Ananie ki baptiza
feit poil: le baptiza

Hic conuisantur opti
mi mercatores q an
tps machometi
mercuriu dm
mercatoru
coluert.

Tute ceste terre ki gut est cuiche est en la seignurie des sarrazins. E entref les autres Sapha
poissantz iueint li uieuz de la muntaine. co est a sau li suuerins de hautz assis. ki por
tent les cureus e ocieue celui dut il cumandemet de lur suuereint. l cele obediece co dient
les sauuera.

Hic s: procul ilsuz borea
manet uetus de
monte.

Hic habundant cameli bubali
muli. asini quib; uruntur
institores int orientales
z occidental es tusme
antes.

Hla tur ayaludite

Hic cimetire
Seie nicholas y ho
entere les morz

Hla porte par...
le ajolu de de...

Le chemin seuf...

le chastel le rei de acre

Hla
vile
de acre

lospital
mans...

la tur de t...

Hla tur de pisanz

Co est le burg kiest apele mistemtard la por te de
Hio est tur le plu fort abure de engloif sont nichola...

la maisun del
hospital sett joha

Ceste uile uaut a sun
seignur chescun
an cinquante
mile liure
dargent.

Ceste cite ki ore est apelee acre
ia apelee tholomaida. Ele est
rance e refui as tuz cristiens
la terre seinte uiue e remendr
pur les sucurs kele a de la me
li uent de ture europe e de tut
isles ken la mer sut e cristien...

Doni militie occe
larari qisst

Le tem
ple